T0360722

Cambridge Elements

Elements in Leadership
edited by
Ronald E. Riggio
Claremont McKenna College
Susan E. Murphy
University of Edinburgh
Founding Editor
Georgia Sorenson
University of Cambridge

PEACE LEADERSHIP

A Story of Peace Dwelling

Stan Amaladas
Baker College

CAMBRIDGE
UNIVERSITY PRESS

Shaftesbury Road, Cambridge CB2 8EA, United Kingdom

One Liberty Plaza, 20th Floor, New York, NY 10006, USA

477 Williamstown Road, Port Melbourne, VIC 3207, Australia

314–321, 3rd Floor, Plot 3, Splendor Forum, Jasola District Centre,
New Delhi – 110025, India

103 Penang Road, #05–06/07, Visioncrest Commercial, Singapore 238467

Cambridge University Press is part of Cambridge University Press & Assessment,
a department of the University of Cambridge.

We share the University's mission to contribute to society through the pursuit of
education, learning and research at the highest international levels of excellence.

www.cambridge.org
Information on this title: www.cambridge.org/9781009543781

DOI: 10.1017/9781009543828

First published 2024

A catalogue record for this publication is available from the British Library.

ISBN 978-1-009-54378-1 Hardback
ISBN 978-1-009-54381-1 Paperback
ISSN 2631-7796 (online)
ISSN 2631-7788 (print)

Cambridge University Press & Assessment has no responsibility for the persistence
or accuracy of URLs for external or third-party internet websites referred to in this
publication and does not guarantee that any content on such websites is, or will
remain, accurate or appropriate.

Peace Leadership

A Story of Peace Dwelling

Elements in Leadership

DOI: 10.1017/9781009543828
First published online: November 2024

Stan Amaladas
Baker College

Author for correspondence: Stan Amaladas, samala02@baker.edu

Abstract: Peace dwelling is formulated as a reciprocal relationship among four interrelated ways of 'Being': Being a Guardian, Being a Curator, Being a Welcoming Presence, and Being a Neighbour. These ways of 'Being' are connected to a systemic reconstruction of Burns' formulation of the essential task of leadership, which encompasses the interconnectedness among the affairs of the Head (consciousness raising because values exist only where there is consciousness), the Heart (feeling the need to meaningfully define values, because where nothing is felt, nothing matters), the Hands (purposeful action), and the Holy (treating persons like persons as a non-negotiable and sacred practice, while believing that all persons can be lifted into their better selves). Corresponding to the four ways of Being, Peace Leadership is interpreted as the art of learning how to properly integrate the affairs of 4-Hs into our own shared lived existence for the sake of dwelling in peace.

Keywords: leadership, peace leadership, peace building, peace dwelling, ecological approach, ecosystemic thinking, guardian, curator, welcoming presence, neighbour

ISBNs: 9781009543781 (HB), 9781009543811 (PB), 9781009543828 (OC)
ISSNs: 2631-7796 (online), 2631-7788 (print)

Contents

A Personal Story

Several weeks after Hamas' 7 October 2023 attack in Israel and Israel's military reaction I was asked to facilitate a workshop on 'Trust-Building in Times of Violence'. All participants were in one way or another, deeply committed to peacebuilding, and peace making. They gathered for a twofold purpose. First, to intentionally look for ways to talk about peace in their own back yards in the face of these horrific events. Second, to engage in the question of how they can best care for themselves and for each other while living in the gap between their aspirations (peace) and what is (violence). Before long, I could simply feel the tensions rise. Voices were raised. Bodies stiffened. Angry comments against Hamas deadly attack and against Israel's unrestrained military reaction were flying all over the place. It was so unlike the people I thought I knew in this room. No one was listening to the other and some were literally finger pointing and talking over (shouting) each other as they charged each other with not understanding. ('No, No, No, you just don't understand!'). I was at a total loss as to what I needed to do. I was stunned at what I was seeing and experiencing. If 'facilitate' means to make (from the Latin, *facere*) easy (from the Latin, *facile*) I was struggling 'to make' what I was experiencing 'easy'. In fact, I simply felt helpless at that moment.

I remember taking a deep breath and asking the Lord for help: 'Please Lord, help me out here!' (Yes, I am a practicing Catholic, and this is what I learned early in my life: 'When in doubt, ask the Lord for His Advice'. I was also cautioned by my Spiritual Advisers: 'You may not like the advice you receive!'). Without planning, and in total spontaneity, I quietly removed myself from this circle, went to a corner of the room, and started to softly (but loud enough for others to hear) sing St. Francis' Prayer of Peace: 'Make Me a Channel of Your Peace'. I honestly could not believe that I was doing this! For fear of breaking down in tears, I did not look at anyone in the circle as I sang the lyrics that I knew, and hummed to the lyrics I didn't. Initially, some stopped shouting at each other and stared at me. Then, one yelled: 'Are you crazy?' I ignored that question. What occurred in this spontaneous process was something also unplanned. It was indeed a pleasant surprise. Some in the circle stopped talking, stayed in their seats, and started to hum and sing that same song/hymn; some joined me in the corner where I stood, and hummed and sang along with me. Tears were rolling down their cheeks. I teared too. Shortly after, silence prevailed as some went to get themselves a glass of water, or a soft drink . . . some hugged others in the room . . . as friends hug each other. At that moment, there was no need for words. It was as if each understood that they all needed to pause and search their own minds, hearts, and souls for the sake of dwelling in peace . . .

Note: The names of participants and the place where this occurred are excluded for the sake of anonymity.

1 Introduction

This Element is written with three goals in mind: (i) to show how we can choose to be with each other in ways that preserves the integrity of each person as a person in peaceful times and in times of disturbance, (ii) to offer tools and a framework to guide peace leaders and followers to dwell in peace, and (iii) to encourage all to seize opportunities to exercise peace leadership that are within their reach. From a methodological perspective, the lived experience of the personal story shared will serve as the context and 'case' or 'incident' for thinking about peace leadership. While this Element will be bounded by the context, interactions, relationships, and responses of this 'incident', it is also intended to serve as a backdrop and an opportunity to engage in an interpretive understanding of peace dwelling within a 'real-world' context. But some might argue: 'surely this micro-event cannot be appropriate, let alone be sufficient, to address very big questions of peace and violence in our real world?' In response to a question like this, I plead with my readers to seriously consider my 'if-then' questions. If we cannot dwell in peace at local and micro levels, then what hope do we have for dwelling in peace at national and international levels or in someone else's back yards? If we cannot dwell in peace wherever we find ourselves, in our Here and Now, then where can we dwell in peace?

A political theorist, Arendt (2018), offers us a way of thinking about our thinking about the use of a case or incident.

> Thought itself – to the extent that it is more than a technical, logical operation . . . – arises out of the actuality of incidents, and incidents of living experience must remain the guideposts by which it takes its bearings if it is not to lose itself in the heights to which thinking soars, or in the depths to which it must descend. (p. 203)

Descriptions and interpretations of this incident or case, then, are such that it must remain bound to this incident. The lived experience within the context of this incident will remain the guideposts to take our bearings for what it means to dwell in peace. The best we can expect is not any formal definitions of peace dwelling, but a discovery that may illuminate our understanding of what it means to dwell in peace.

The language of *dwelling* places us within the space of home and by implication, homelessness. Our everyday use of the language of home, offer us different images of what it means to feel or be-at-home. For example, gracious hosts, invite their guests into their homes with: 'Make yourselves at Home'. Returning from a vacation, we hear many say: 'Home Sweet Home'. We hear our loved ones say: 'Welcome Home.' We also hear that 'Home is where the Heart Is'. While away from home, we hear some as longing for 'the green, green grass of home', and others as acknowledging being in a 'home away from home'. Being at home then resonates with different images of genuinely experiencing (a) like we belong, (b) a longing for home, (c) relaxation, (d) the freedom to enjoy being in the presence and hospitality of gracious hosts, (e) gratefulness to the point where guests return the graciousness of hosts with respect and appreciation, (f) being uninhibited to be who we are without judgement, (g) feeling safe and secure from any threat of danger, (h) *as if* we are in the presence of family and friends.

In being disturbed by the violence in the Middle East, participants in this 'incident' began to dwell in that space in ways that only increased their experience of restlessness and anxiety (being-not-at-home). A philosopher like Heidegger (1995) affirms that this interaction of being-at-home (state of rest) and being-not-at home (restlessness) is a part of our human condition – they are both a part of our human experience. (p. 5). For him restlessness is a human affirmation that we are 'not-at-home' everywhere and every time. Similarly, we read a hermeneutic-philosopher and phenomenologist, Gadamer (1996a) interpreting the philosopher Hegel in this way:

> The expression of 'making oneself at home in the world' was a favourite one of Hegel's and he regarded it as constitutive of what it means to be human. It describes the desire to be at home with oneself, secure from any threat of danger, surrounded by a familiar, understood, and understandable world where one can feel free of anxiety. (p. 154)

1.1 What's the Problem?

The problem of peace dwelling as suggested by Hegel and Heidegger is that it is more than having a roof over our heads or building structures for habitation. Without disavowing the need to have a roof over our heads, for both these philosophers, the desire to make oneself at home in our world is constitutive of what it means to be human. The desire to feel secure from any threat of danger and being surrounded by a familiar, understood, and understandable world, appear to resonate with the different images of being-at-home as presented earlier. However, unlike Gadamer's formulation of the philosopher Hegel 'where one can feel free of anxiety', for Heidegger, anxiety or what he calls 'restlessness', by virtue of being a human condition, means that we are not and cannot be 'free of anxiety'. To be free of anxiety is to be free from what it means to be a human being. This does not mean that as human beings we are simply condemned to a life of restlessness. Dwelling in peace within the context of being-at-home and being-not-at-home means that we need to begin by acknow-ledging that we dwell in an *in-between space* of restlessness (being-not-at-home) and feeling like we belong (being-at-home). If we accept this then the problem and question of dwelling in peace is a matter of addressing a question that is rooted in our human condition: *How can we dwell decisively and imaginatively in this in-between space of being-at-home and being-not-at-home?*

1.2 A Shift in Thinking

The problem of peace dwelling, as it is reflected in this question, differs from what we learn from scholars within our emerging field called peace leadership. For example, in an interview with Mexiner (2006), a well-respected leadership scholar Dr Jean Lipman-Blumen[1] raised the question 'leadership for 'what?' It was a question that was already raised by Burns (1978) whom some consider as the father of leadership studies (Barbour, 2006): 'Leadership for *what* end?' (Burns, 1978, p. 457; emphasis original). This question presupposes a genuine interest in claiming the purpose of leadership. For Lipman-Blumen,

> As educators, we must ask, 'leadership for what?' That is the basic question! It is not about the leaders; it is what the leaders have to solve. If we can make leadership programs problem-focused instead of person-focused, that would be a very important leap forward. What do you want to *make better* in this society?' (Mexiner, 2006, p. 4; emphasis original)

A story is also told that Lipman-Blumen answered the 'leadership for what?' question at an International Leadership Association (ILA) Conference: 'Leadership for what, if not for peace' (McIntyre Miller, 2016). If we stayed with Lipman-Blumen's formulation of leaders as problem-solvers ('it is what leaders have to solve'), it could appear as if peace leaders are being called upon to be problem-focused by solving or fixing the problem of violence. This may be how problem-solvers make whatever they want to *make better* in society. If this is indeed so, then dwelling in peace would become a technical and logical operation – an activity that may be more appropriate for electronic machines rather than the human brain – to solve an 'unhealthy' problem like restlessness. But is this what's really at stake? Gadamer's (1996b), formulation of the 'enigma' of health, may help us understand the problem differently.

---

[1] Among other things, Lipman-Blumen is the author of *The Allure of Toxic Leadership,* Professor of Organizational Behavior at Claremont Graduate University's Peter F. Drucker and Masatoshi Ito Graduate School of Management, former Thornton F. Bradshaw Professor of Public Policy, and founder of the Connective Leadership Institute.

We need to recognize that it is only through a disturbance of the whole that a genuine consciousness of the problem and a genuine concentration of thought upon it can arise ... But of course it is the state of being healthy which possesses ontological primacy, that natural condition of life which we term well-being ... But what is well-being if not precisely this condition of not noticing, of being unhindered, of being ready and open to everything? (p. 73)

This understanding of well-being has also filtered into political life in Greek literature. As Gadamer (1996b) shared,

Plato's great utopia of the *Republic* the true part of the citizen ... is described in terms of health, as a harmony in which everything is in accord, in which the fateful problem of governing and being governed is resolved through reciprocal agreement and mutual interaction. (p. 75)

Restlessness and anxiety especially amid human conditions of violence suggests that the 'well-being' of the whole is disturbed, and that everything is not in accord. It is indeed revealing to also note that the World Churches Council (2012), also talked about peace from the perspective of 'wholeness' and to the well-being of the whole (p. 26). Gadamer's formulation of the 'enigma' of health offers us another way of understanding the problem raised in this Element. As he shared, well-being by virtue of <u>being well</u>, expresses itself through a condition of not noticing, of being unhindered, and of being ready and open to everything. In being well or healthy (or being-at-home), we are unhindered by thoughts of illness (or being-not-at-home). When we are in good health, we are genuinely absorbed in what we are doing. Being undisturbed, being healthy, or being well, offers us the gift of 'not noticing' illness or restlessness. Health offers us the gift to freely participate in our everyday lives and engage with others in ways that are unhindered by illness (or feeling restless). In being well or healthy, the gift of health – of not noticing and being unhindered by illness or restlessness – however, does not mean that we forget about illness or restlessness. Instead, for Gadamer, well-being is received as preparing us to be ready and open to everything. Paradoxically, the 'enigmatic' gift of well-being, and in our context, being-at-home is that it while it frees us from not noticing and being unhindered by concerns of being-not-at-home, it also prepares us to be ready and open to noticing in times of disturbance.

1.3 Enigma of Peace Dwelling

We could also say that herein lies the 'enigma' of peace dwelling: that is only through a disturbance of the well-being of the whole or a disturbance in harmony where everything is not in accord, that we can become genuinely conscious of the problem of peace dwelling and show a genuine concentration of thought upon peace. Within the context of peace dwelling, Gadamer (1996) could be interpreted as saying that what is really at stake is that we are all called not to solve the problem of disturbance/restlessness, or to think that the task before us is to eliminate disturbance/restlessness, but rather to reflect upon and be thoughtful about it means to dwell decisively in this in-between place of peace (being-at-home) and disturbance/restlessness (being-not-at-home). While a distinction is made between being-at-home and being not-an-home, this does not mean that they are dichotomous. This distinction surfaces instead a reality that draws us into a delicate balancing act.

Undoubtedly, this question, problem, and reflection belong to all who find themselves in the middle of being disturbed. In being disturbed by violence, decisions and choices need to be made. Allow me to revert to the 'incident' which I offered in the opening pages of this Element. In retrospect, a critical learning is that the decision to step away from that space of noise, acrimony, and restlessness enabled the presencing or the appearance of a 'pleasant surprise'. Returning to Gadamer (1996), he could now be heard as saying that well-being or being-at-home, could potentially prepare us to be open to the possibility of being surprised in times of disturbance. Does this mean that such 'pleasant surprises' are guaranteed? No. Why? Because we don't know what will happen when we initiate something new. We simply cannot know. Such is the nature of any initiative. We may be surprised. We may be disappointed. As the lyrics of a song, *Que Cera, Cera* goes: *The future's not ours to see . . . what will be, will be.*

At the same time, while the future consequences of our initiative may not be ours to see, can we not give ourselves the gift of imagining alternatives and possibilities other than shouting and finger-pointing, (blaming) in moments of restlessness and disturbance? What is for us to see, then, are choices and decisions that we can make from the perspective of our imagined alternatives and possibilities amid disturbances. With regard to the personal story shared, it is only in retrospect that we come to know that the actions taken at <u>that</u> disturbance ('incident'), opened <u>that</u> dwelling space *to evolve* from a 'normalcy' of how we are supposed to act in an acrimonious state, to confusion, to a charge of 'being crazy' – a charge that takes its own bearings from what it means to act normally under such conditions of disturbance – to the surprise of others joining in and embracing such a 'craziness' for the sake of peace dwelling. What is important to note is that the experience of 'surprise' and being open to being surprised cannot take its bearings from what reacting normally to disturbances has come to mean. It is indeed the decision to step out of this normal-crazy socially constructed convention that enables the possibility of being surprised.

If peace is indeed the purpose of leadership, and if this is expressed as a concern for what we 'want to *make better* in this society', then this desire is interpreted as being deeply connected to the *problem* and the *question* of what it means to dwell decisively in our in-between space of being-at-home and being-not-at-home by being open to being surprised by the appearance of new possibilities. To suggest that we need to make something *better*, presupposes that we have not done a good job in responding to this problem and question. Said differently, we may not have done a good job in preparing ourselves to stay open to the surprise that there may be possibilities other than reacting to violence with counter-violence. This is a theoretical, philosophical, and practical problem confronting peace dwellers. Practical, not in terms of 'how-to' and rather as 'practice' which is understood as a 'choice and decision between possibilities' and as 'always [having] a relationship to a person's being' (Gadamer, 1996c, pp. 3–4).

Restlessness and the suffering or pain that it inflicts change in character when they are no longer accompanied by the certainty or expectation that restlessness can be eliminated or that peace leadership is about solving the problem of restlessness. What is at stake in the presence of restlessness is that peace dwellers are called to be decisively imaginative in terms of choosing between different possibilities including a decision with regard to who one chooses to be in times of disturbance (relationship to one's being). Consequently, it is not a matter of condoning violence, reacting to violence, solving violence, or giving violence the last word. It is a matter of being open to being surprised by new possibilities amid conditions of disturbance and restlessness.

The experience of violence and counter-violence in the Middle East is such that discord rather than harmony is what it is because both sides of the conflict (Hamas and Netanyahu's government) have mutually resolved to destroy each other. They are locked in and imprisoned by their reactions of violence and counter-violence. Each side of the conflict has chosen to govern and be governed by the principles of hate and revenge, disguised, and rationalized as their right to assure security for themselves. Within the context of the experience in the 'incident' of the personal story, participants at that workshop chose to express their anger and frustration by shouting and talking over others because of what they saw and experienced as injustice. They were disturbed by the injustice of Hobbes' (1651/1977) *Leviathan* formulation of human life in its natural state, namely that human life is reduced to being 'solitary, poor, nasty, brutish, and short' (p. 100). This state of brutishness, as Hobbes (1642/2017) proclaimed in *De Cive* is grounded in mutual fear rather than mutual love. Politically, in this state of mutual fear, 'every man is enemy to every man … wherein men live without other security than what their own strength … shall furnish them withal' (Hobbes, 1651/1977, p. 100).

This 'continued state' of mutual fear excludes any hope that there can be new alternatives or possibilities. A life without hope is a life of constant restlessness, of mutual fear in the ill-will of others, of misery, and of feeling abandoned. It is a life that is constrained and imprisoned by a view of the other as an enemy and as an entity that is separated and disconnected from other human beings. A life without hope is a life that affirms it is indeed solitary, poor, nasty, and brutish. While Hobbes affirmed that this condition is true for a life in its natural state, namely a life without 'society' or 'government' (Hobbes, 1651/1977), his notion of government is interpreted as governance. In this way, hope and imagination offers one answer to our research question and problem of what it means to dwell decisively in the in-between space of violence and peace. We can choose to dwell decisively in this in-between space by surrendering ourselves to being governed *by the spirit of hope and imagination*.

Within the context of the 'case' or 'incident 'presented, the absence of hope and the imagination of new possibilities sustains the impossibility of being surprised by the possibility that relationships could be other than what it is between participants in that story and in the larger story between Palestinians and Israelis. This impossibility was already encapsulated in a refusal to pay attention to Jen Anders Toyberg-Frandzen's plea. As the interim Assistant-Secretary-General for UN Political Affairs, about ten years ago, he noted:

> The continued reality of the close to 50-year long occupation and the lack of progress towards the two-State solution ensure that the next round of violence is never too far below the surface. The time has come for leaders on both sides to make the difficult compromises that will promote stability and ensure long-term security for both Israelis and Palestinians. (United Nations, 2014, para 2)

Toyberg-Frandzen's plea needs to be taken in context. The Human Rights Watch (2013) reported:

> Serious violations of international human rights and humanitarian law continued in 2012 in Israel and in the West Bank and Gaza. Renewed armed conflict between Israel and Hamas and armed groups in Gaza from November 14–21 involved unlawful attacks on civilians by both sides ... In the West Bank, including East Jerusalem, Israeli settlers injured 151 Palestinians as of November 27, Israel imposed severe restrictions on Palestinians' right to freedom of movement, continued to build unlawful settlements in occupied territory, and arbitrarily detained Palestinians, including children and peaceful protesters. (para 1 & 2)

We notice the consequences of a toxic recursive relationship playing itself out for both Israelis and Palestinians then, and now. Bateson (1979), an anthropologist and systems thinker, distinguished lineal and recursive relationships in the following way: '*Lineal* describes a relationship among a series of causes or arguments such that the sequence does not came back to the starting point . . . . The opposite of *lineal* is *recursive*' (p. 228; emphasis in original). Sadly, it appears as if Toyberg-Frandzen's political plea 'to make the difficult compromises' and to engage in the process of developing a 'two-state solution' have fallen on deaf-ears and it makes peace among Israelis and Palestinians seem like an eternal impossibility. Because the actions of both parties return to their 'starting point' (enmity) the tensions that lay 'never too far below the surface' has simply bubbled over, like a volcanic eruption, and it is burning with rage. In this context, it is not the experience of 'home sweet home' but rather the experience of restlessness and disturbance that seems to prevail. In this context, hopelessness prevails because the no-longer questioned 'starting point' of a life of mutual fear, or a view of the other as an enemy, and a refusal to make difficult compromises for the sake of a two-state solution, continue to perpetuate a relationship of violence and counter-violence.

1.4 Relationship Is the Practice of Leadership

Within our 'emerging discipline' called Leadership Studies (Riggio, 2011), Burns (1978, 2003) offered us a way to conceptualize the practical work and the practice of leadership in the context of peace-dwelling. To be clear, while he spoke to leadership, he did not directly address peace dwelling. Burns (1978) distinguished the practice of leadership from the action(s) of any one person. He viewed the practice of leadership from the perspective of 'a *relationship* between leaders and a multitude of followers' (Burns, 1978, p. 30; emphasis original) where 'leaders take the initiative in mobilizing people for participation in the processes of change' (Burns, 2003, p. 25). Second, he conceptualized transforming leadership within the context of such a mobilization. He outlined his 'core agenda for transforming leadership' as 'leaders working as partners with the dispossessed of the world to secure life, liberty, and happiness – happiness empowered with transforming purpose . . .' (Burns, 2003, p. 3). Could we not also add, leaders and followers working as partners with all to dwell in peace – peace empowered with a transforming purpose?

1.5 Not Leader-Centric

Peace leadership, then, is not about traits or skills of any one person. It is not person-centric as ascribed by Carlyle (1841/1993) and other traits (Kirkpatrick and Locke, 1991; Zaccaro, 2007), and skills-based (Katz, 1955; Mumford et al., 2000; Yammarino, 2000) approaches to the study of leadership. However, while the concept of relationship-oriented behaviour has been around since the early days of leadership studies, Uhl-Bien (2006) noted that 'the term *relational leadership* is surprisingly new' (p. 654). While it is indeed encouraging to note that there is a growing list of leadership scholars who are embracing and studying leadership as leaders and followers standing in a socially constructed relationship with each other (Graen and Uhl-Bien, 1995, 2005; Heifetz and Linsky, 2017; Kouzes and Posner, 2017; Popper, 2004; Scandura and Meuser, 2022), a dominant positivistic paradigm continues to prevail in our discourse about leadership.

For example, Bateson (2000) noted in the Preface to a later edition of her father's *Steps to an Ecology of Mind,* that Western epistemology drives men and women to (a) 'search for short term solutions that worsen the problem over time (often by mirroring it, such as violence used to oppose violence)' and (b) 'focus on individual persons or organisms or even species . . . in isolation' (p. xiv) from each other and from context. She further went on to say that 'even with current progress in chaos and complexity theory, we remain less skilled at thinking about interactions than we are at thinking about entities, things' (Bateson, 2000, p. vii; parenthesis original). In sociology, Durkheim's (1966) proposition . . . that social facts (including peace) are to be treated as 'things' (p. 14; parenthesis added), appears to not only rule the scientific-positivistic sociological method, but also how we approach our study of leadership. This positivistic method excludes thinking about the implications of interactions and relationships as subsystems within larger systems which may have an investment in maintaining levels of restlessness.

1.6 Peace Is Not a 'Thing'

To think of peace as a 'thing' is to orient to actions like peace building or peace making. It is to think of peace as a 'thing' that can be built, crafted or fabricated. Within the field of peace and conflict, peace building is generally conceptualized as a movement 'toward a frame of reference that focuses on the restoration and rebuilding of relationships' (Lederach, 2017, p. 24). Restorations and rebuilding occur after the end of violence, when all in conflict choose to put their 'swords' down. What is dropped from this dominant *homo-faber* focus is to think about peace dwelling as a human relationship between being-at-home (a state of rest) and being-not-at-home (a state of restlessness) – especially when we fall outside this place of caring for how we choose to dwell with each other. The significance of thinking and talking about peace dwelling rather than peace building is that something decisive is concealed in peace building. For Heidegger (1977), what is concealed in peace-building is that 'dwelling is not experienced as man's Being; dwelling is never thought of as the basic character of human being' (p. 326). Thinking of peace leadership from the vantage point of peace dwelling is a way of revealing how humans can <u>choose to be</u> in this in-between space of being-at-home (a state-of-rest) and being-not-at-home (a state-of-restlessness).

1.7 Moving Forward

In the section that follows, a fourfold conceptual peace-leadership framework is offered to aid us in addressing the problem and the question confronting peace dwellers as that was raised in the preceding pages. To this end, a deliberate attempt is made to reconstruct Burns' (1978) formulation of the 'fundamental act of the leader' while keeping in mind that leadership is a relationship and partnership among leaders and followers who seek to dwell in peace.

Second, the life and lived experience of peace dwellers are discussed through four metaphors. *Guardian*: Following the philosopher Heidegger (1977), who formulated peace dwelling as being brought to peace and remaining at peace by caring for, sparing and safeguarding each other from harm and danger, these values and actions are collected under the rubric of being a Guardian. *Curator*: The complexity of embodying Guardianship within the context of violence that we witness in our world today is such that we find ourselves in the middle of betrayal, distrust, and dehumanizing practices that stand in the way of dwelling in peace and remaining at peace. Within this context, peace dwellers as Curators of hearts and souls are offered as a metaphor to enable being at peace with oneself and others amid such betrayals and distrust. *Welcoming Presence*: Here, the question of how peace dwellers can be a welcoming presence to self and others amid conditions of disturbance and violence is discussed in some detail. Finally, *Being a Neighbour:* Being a neighbour is discussed through the notion of 'habit' or practiced conduct of 'making oneself available' (Ricouer, 1965, p. 95) to others where they are, including being present to the wounded, to the dispossessed, and to those who are hurting.

2 A Fourfold Conceptual Framework for Peace Leadership

As experienced in the incident for this Element, after those in the room joined their facilitator in singing or humming to the Peace song, silence prevailed. There was no need for words. What can we make of the participants' silence? Silence can be (is?) a powerful tool for listening. Perhaps it is not accidental that the words 'listen' and 'silent' are composed of the same alphabets – albeit rearranged. Brox (2019), for example, remarked: 'To fully listen requires silence. To engage in meaningful conversation requires silence' (p. 70). For Brox, 'silence' does not lead to action-paralysis but rather it is valued because it offers speakers an opportunity to 'pause to think', and 'to choose the right word'

(p. 70). 'The silence in which another listens,' she added, 'is a sign of respect that allows time to comprehend the weight and meaning of what is said' (p. 70). As some moved to quenching their thirst, their silence communicated an acknowledgement that they all needed to pause and search their own minds, hearts, and souls for the sake of dwelling in peace.

In this respect, it is revealing to hear Burns (1978) as also formulating the task of a leader through the lenses of the head and the heart.

> Essentially the leader's task is consciousness-raising on a wide plane. 'Values exist only when there is consciousness,' Susanne Langer has said. 'Where noting is felt, nothing matters.' The leader's fundamental act is to induce people to be aware or conscious of what they feel, to feel their needs so strongly, to define their values so meaningfully, that they can be moved to purposeful action. (Burns, 1978, pp. 43–44)

Burns (1978) introduced us to three 'core' tasks of the leader. The first task, consciousness-raising is interpreted as being an affair of the **Head** (Mind). The term 'consciousness-raising' was popularized by a Brazilian educator, activist, and critical theorist, Paulo Freire (1970) in his book *Pedagogy of the Oppressed*. Consciousness-raising, and in particular education for critical consciousness (*conscientzação* – in Portuguese) underlies Freire's revolutionary method of education. It is an education that aims at moving all to strive for their own humanity by changing structures and systems that dehumanize both the oppressor and the oppressed. It is in this way that we also understand the Head as calling us to change our socially constructed and structured ways of thinking about peace. While that may be consciousness raising on a wide plane, Burns appears to have something more specific in mind. In citing Susanne Langer, 'values exist only where there is consciousness', for Burns (1978) consciousness raising is the art of becoming aware of values rooted in and guiding the practice of leadership – and for us, peace leadership. To be unaware of values guiding leadership practices is to be in the world like a sleepwalker – asleep and oblivious. By implication, becoming conscious of values can only occur in our state of wakefulness.

In this state of wakefulness, the second task is to 'to induce people to be aware or conscious of what they feel, to feel their needs so strongly, to define their values so meaningfully . . .' But why the need induce people to be aware or conscious of what they feel? As Burns (1978) cited Susanne Langer again, it is because 'where nothing is felt nothing matters' (p. 44). Where nothing matters, indifference prevails. It is because some things matter that it becomes necessary to meaning-fully define their values. In this way, the manner in which participants in the incident conducted themselves is itself an expression of what they felt and valued.

They felt that the destruction of human lives were simply unacceptable. If this meant nothing to them, then there will be no place for caring about the problem of dwelling well in this in-between place when confronted with any disturbance or disharmony. There will also be no place for being disturbed. If indifference is not to prevail, then, for the sake of dwelling in peace, this group of participants would be required to feel the need to meaningfully define the values underlying their anger and feeling disturbed. A similar call to feel the need to meaningfully define our values, was passionately expressed by Marx (1856/1978) when he reflected on the glory and pain of industrialization in the nineteenth century: 'But although the atmosphere in which we live weighs upon everyone like a 20,000 lb. force, do you *feel* it?' (p. 577; emphasis added). It is as if Marx also understood in his heart of hearts, that if nothing is *felt*, nothing matters. If nothing matters, then indifference would be a societal way of being in the world. This second task is offered here as being the affair of the **H**eart.

Third, Burns (1978) noted that both consciousness raising and inducing others to feel the need to meaningfully define their values (including anger), stand in a relationship to 'purposeful action' ('that they can be moved to purposeful action'). Burns' use of *purposeful action* is interpreted not from the perspective of an instrumental or calculative means to an end, but rather from the perspective of Weber (1968), the sociologist's formulation of *value-rational action*. According to Weber (1978), value rational action is 'determined by a conscious belief in the value for its own sake . . . independently of its prospects for success' (pp. 24–25). If this is so, then, as will be raised later in this Element, unlike Burns' claim, the effectiveness of leadership cannot be 'measured' or 'tested by results' (Burns, 2003, p. 3). Suffice for now to say that an image of purposeful action is offered through the metaphor of the **H**ands.

Within the field of leadership studies, several leadership scholars are familiar with connecting the work of leadership through the metaphors of the Head and Heart (Kouzes and Posner, 2017), Head, Heart and Hands (Nicholls, 1994) and others, like Staub ll (1997), have written exclusively on the Heart of Leadership. The 3-Hs of leadership work, relate to the questions of what we need to *know* (Head: consciousness-raising, knowing what values are governing our choices), how we need to *be* (Heart: to feel the need to meaningfully define how we choose to be with each other because where nothing is felt, nothing matters) and what we need to *do* (Hands: be moved to a value rational purposeful action).

Burns (1978), however, does not stop there. He concluded his volume on *Leadership,* by connecting the fundamental task of leadership to his 'practical advice' – to yet another value – 'treat all persons like *persons*' (Burns, 1978, p. 462; emphasis original) and not like pawns or things to be manipulated, enslaved, controlled, discarded, dehumanized, or killed. In this, he shares in the philosopher Immanuel Kant's call that we must treat others 'always ... as an end' (Kant, 1785/1956, p. 6). As he closed his volume on *Leadership*, he grounded the transforming work of leadership in a belief/value that 'people can be lifted *into* their better selves' (Burns, 1978, p. 462; emphasis original). Treating persons like *persons*, as a 'Thou', and not as an 'It' (Buber, 1970), is interpreted as a principled, sacred, and non-negotiable gift that persons give to each other and owe one another. Within the context of restlessness and violence, it is a gift and a debt that is rooted in a belief 'that people can be lifted *into* their better selves.

In this manner, a psychologist, Kornfield (1993) noted that 'community is created when people come together not in the name of religion, but when they come together bringing honesty, respect, and kindness to support an awakening of the sacred' (p. 24), and, as Heifetz and Linksy (2017) noted, when people lead with an open and 'sacred heart' (p. 227). Accordingly, Burns' practical advice, belief, and value/principle are placed in the spiritual realm of a fourth H – the **H**oly. The concept of 'holy' is used here not in the name of religion, but rather in a deeply humanistic and spiritual context. It is akin to Marx's (1848/1978) lament in the age of industrialization: 'All that is Solid melts into air ... all that is holy is profaned' (p. 476) because human beings neglected their interpersonal responsibility to each other by reducing some to simply being an 'appendage of a machine' (p. 479). In this way, Marx could be interpreted as summoning the need to not only think about what we are doing, but also to feel the need to think about our thinking about what we are doing.

2.1 Epistemology of Peace Dwelling

The epistemology grounding peace dwelling is interpreted as the dynamic and reciprocal nature of the fourfold oneness of peace leadership's purposes of the head, heart, hands, and holy. As a fourfold, all four Hs are received as being interconnected and interrelated to each other. They are not and cannot be separated from each other. Imagine peace dwelling in the absence of any one H. Within the context of the fourfold it doesn't make sense to talk about crossing boundaries. In the fourfold, we have instead a 'mix' or a 'combination' of the dynamic interrelated oneness of the fourfold that is both distinct and connected. The interconnectedness of the fourfold, means that each *H* thinks of and orients to the other three *H*s along with itself in everything each of the Hs do. Figure 1 visualizes the interactions and interconnectedness of the four Hs of peace leadership.

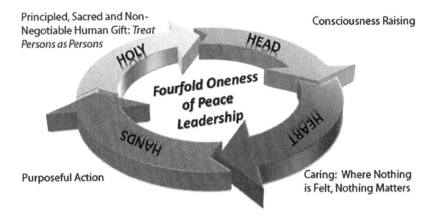

Figure 1 Fourfold oneness of peace leadership

2.1.1 On the Significance of the Number 4

Our human language is filled with descriptions of a sense of 'completeness' with the number 4. Four winds; Four directions; Four seasons; Four ancient rivers from the Old Testament (Pishon, Gihon, Tigris, and Euphrates); Four rivers in Hindu scripture (Ganges, Indus, Oxus, and Śita); Four alphabets for the name of God in Hebrew: YHWH; Four elements; Four Houses in J.K. Rowling's *Harry Potter*, each house representing one of the four elements. Gryffindor (Fire), Hufflepuff (Earth), Ravenclaw (Air), Slytherin (Water); Four states of matter; Four limbs of the human body; Four phases of the moon; and so forth. In Chinese culture because the word for the number 4 '*si*' is also contained in the word '*Sîwáng*' which means death, such a number is considered unlucky.

Through a Jungian lens, four is known as the *quaternity* and is traditionally understood as a symbol of totality, stability, wholeness, and completeness. Joseph Campbell (1949) spelt out four purposes of myth, (a) spiritual: relating to the mystery of the world in which we live, (b) cosmological: a meaningful understanding of our natural world and having an appropriate relationship with it, (c) moral: establishing and living our lives in an ethical way, and (d) psychological: living a meaningful life in relation to nature and society. Thomas Moore (2009) offered his understanding of what it means to be a Christian through his integrated oneness of four ways of being (a) *metanoia*, a fundamental change of mind and heart, (b) *basilea*, understood as the kingdom of God that is not up above but within each and everyone of us, (c) *agape,* charity as the highest form of love and (d) *therapeia*, the art of healing. Martin Heidegger (1977) spoke to the '*primal oneness of the four – earth, sky, divinities, and mortal – belonging together in one*' (p. 327). After surviving her bout with lung cancer, the poet Mary Oliver (2014) concluded her poem 'The Fourth Sign of the Zodiac' with a fourfold blessing:

Bless the feet that take you to and fro.
Bless the eyes and the listening ears.
Bless the tongue, the marvel of taste.
Bless touching. (p. 63)

2.2 Look for Patterns Which Connect

In all of the examples offered, we notice both a special place of the number 4 in our human constructions and that neither one of any four stand independent from each other. They are interconnected. Each is understood in their interrelationship with the other. But herein lies a particular challenge with dominant Western epistemology – namely, 'how we can know anything' (p. 4), or 'how knowing is *done* (Bateson and Bateson, 1987, p. 20; emphasis original). Together with his daughter Mary Catherine Bateson, they described how knowing is done in the Western world (Scientific Mind). Scientific minds first 'name the parts' and 'after that the relations between the parts appear as predicates attached usually to a single part – not to the two or more parts among which the relation existed' (Bateson and Bateson, 1987, p. 37). What is dropped from sight is an epistemology that orients to 'a pattern which connects' (Bateson and Bateson, 1987, p. 8) among two or more parts. These authors were guided by an underpinning Oriental (Flemons, 1991) and Indigenous (Lopez, 2020) epistemology, namely, an epistemology of connectedness. It is not, however, a connectedness that erases the distinctions and the spaces between the four Hs but rather, as the Lebanese-American poet Kahlil Gibran (1923/2020) advised those who are married, it is to: ' . . . let there be spaces in your togetherness . . . And stand together yet not too near together' (pp. 15–16).

2.3 Ecological Connectedness of the Fourfold

If leadership is indeed a relationship, then what is particularly inviting is Bateson's call to situate our consciousness of peace leadership within an ecological connectedness of the fourfold. The language of 'eco' in ecology returns us to the notion of home (being-at-home/being not-at-home). While the Greek word for 'eco' – *oikos* means home, for Gadamer (1996b), it means something more. For him, 'it included not only the ability to manage by oneself but also the ability to manage along with other people' (p. 79). He shared that one way we can manage along with others, or dwell in peace, for that matter, 'is to learn properly how to integrate this reliance on one another into our own lived existence' (p. 79). Similarly, peace leadership is interpreted as the art of learning how to properly integrate the four Hs into our own shared lived existence for the sake of dwelling in peace.

2.4 Dominance of Either/Or Thinking

For far too long the mental model of Western epistemology has been dominated by a dualistic either-or thinking. For an organizational learning theorist, Senge (2006), mental models 'are deeply ingrained assumptions, generalizations, or even pictures or images that influence how we understand the world and how we take action' (p. 8). We are accustomed to think in terms of either black or white, either us or them, and so forth. This heady either-or thinking has led some in the field of leadership studies to claim that 'Leadership is not an affair of the head. Leadership is an affair of the heart' (Kouzes and Posner, 2017, p. 313). This bifurcation has also opened problematic either-or debates around head vs heart approaches to leadership and also calls to balance head and heart (Bartimote, 2020; Love, 2005).

The conceptual framework that frames peace leadership for the value rational purpose of dwelling in peace (as an end in itself) suggests that only when peace leadership students, scholars, and practitioners gather with a view to raising their consciousness to the dynamic and reciprocal value-relationship among the four-fold, can we begin to gather with a mutually shared purpose (Amaladas, 2019). Allow me now to turn to my attention to the four distinct, yet interconnected, parts of the fourfold in their combined and mixed relationship to peace dwelling.

3 Leadership as an Affair of the Head: On Being a Guardian

As shared earlier, a 'core' practice of the **H**ead of peace leadership is *both* a consciousness-raising on a wide plane *and* a particular focus on defining values governing peace leadership. While 'consciousness-raising' was understood by Freire (1970) as moving all to strive for their own humanity by changing structures and systems that dehumanize both the oppressor and the oppressed, Burns (1978) could be interpreted as calling us to change our socially constructed ways of thinking about what it means to dwell in peace. How then has peace been understood over time? What values underlie such understandings? What would those defined values mean for peace leadership and for those who choose to dwell in peace?

In asking these questions, it will be wise to recall Gadamer's (1996b) understanding of how language is used: 'In the living use of language, words never exist in isolation. Their meaning is sustained and determined through the proximity and influence of neighbouring words ... neighbouring expressions ... At the same time, however, they are not identical with it' (p. 45). We come to know peace, in other words, by making distinctions and by distinguishing peace through the use of neighbouring words or expressions, while being conscious that the use of the latter are not identical with 'peace'. What then do we know about different formulations and characterizations (neighbouring words, neighbouring expressions) of peace? What are their implications for peace leadership and dwelling in peace?

3.1 Peace as a Preventing Violence

Shortly after World War II, authors of the Constitution of UNESCO (1945), declared that 'since wars begin in the minds of men (and women), it is in the minds of men that the defences of peace must be constructed' (para 1; parenthesis added). Writing within the context of the Vietnam War, Merton (1976) also called on his readers 'to recognize the great problem of the *mental climate* in which we live' whereby our 'minds are filled with images which call for violent and erratic reactions' (p. 17; emphasis original). In stating that 'the defences of peace' must be reconstructed in the minds of men and women, the authors of the 1945 Constitution of UNESCO began with the value of peace as preventing violence. The military language of 'defences' suggests that we dwell in peace by strategically preventing violence. How are we to receive UNESCO's 1945 declaration of what Galtung (1964), a peace and conflict scholar, defined as negative peace?

From the perspective of systems theory, we read that peace is compared and contrasted against that which is not peace – violence/war. For systems theorists like Watzlawick et al. (2011), concepts like peace and violence/war 'stand in a relationship with one another and need to be combined together, in spite of their apparently opposite nature' (p. 3). This is one way through which we have come to know what dwelling in peace means. For these authors, this is 'not an abstruse idea, but a specific instance of the general principle that all perception and thought is relative, operating by comparison and contrast' (Watzlawick et al., 2011, p. 3). Flemons (1991) would further suggest that these concepts belong together and that we can only begin to understand one by understanding the other. Becvar and Becvar (2018) also noted that while these humanly constructed concepts and distinctions (peace/war; positive/ negative), describe two different kinds of social relationships, they are complementary, and this 'complementarity . . . describes one concept rather than two' (p. 15). They are concepts and ways of living that imply an interdependent relationship. What is particularly at stake for systems theorists are two questions whenever they observe a person, a family or a wider social system enmeshed in conflict in persistent and repetitive ways, despite the desire and effort to alter or change such a situation: (i) How does this undesirable situation (conflict/violence) persist?' and (ii) 'What is required to change it?' These questions are relevant because for systems theorists change stands in a relationship with persistence.

One way that persons within nations have proceeded to change the persistence of conflict and war, one response to prevent war is to deter war by building and increasing the production of armaments of war. In this context, the central message of deterrence is to credibly communicate threats of military action or nuclear punishment on the adversary despite its costs to the deterrer. It is a message that relies enthusiastically on an adage derived from a military writer, Vegetius, in Roman times: 'if you want peace, prepare for war' (as cited in Moloney and Williams, 2017, p. 1). In recent times, Glaser (1990) went so far as to rationalize deterrence theory by reducing it to a mathematical/economic equation. Here is how it works. If the attacker believed that the Probability of deterrer carrying out deterrent threats x Costs if threat is carried out is > Probability of the attacker accomplishing the action × Benefits of the action – then attacks will be deterred. This mode is frequently simplified as: Violence will be deterred if attackers believe that Costs × P(Costs) > Benefits × P(Benefits).

If this is indeed true, then how can we explain Hamas' 7 October 2023 undeterred attack on Israel? How can we explain Russia's unprovoked attack against Ukraine? The attackers in these instances have not accomplished their intended objectives and the 'costs' of their actions are far outweighing the 'benefits'. While the unrestrained military reaction against not only Hamas but against all Palestinians may demonstrate Israel's show of force in avenging the terrorists acts, they are now accused of their 'barbaric' military reaction 'without political considerations' (Gillespie and Patman, 2023, para 6). It appears as if all sides of these conflicts are perfectly aligned for the results they are getting. It is not a question of what they are not doing. Instead, it is matter of what they *are* doing.

A question must be asked: 'What happens after the liquidation of Palestinians in the Gaza strip?' Or for that matter, 'what happens after the liquidation of Israelis?' Will either of them (assuming that at least one survived) be perceived as a credible partner in the pursuit of any long-term aspiration for regional or world peace? Will they be respected or viewed as worthy of credibility in any public round table that is focused on peace dwelling? Will not their unrestrained, indiscriminate, disproportionate, and inhumane military reaction be historically viewed as the official representatives of Israel, or Hamas, simply not wanting Palestinians or Israelis anywhere on what they have claim to be 'their' land, and that they really have no use, let alone respect, for Palestinians or Israelis? For all involved in this conflict, in attempts to change conditions of violence, are they themselves not ensuring that such violence persists indeterminately?

To persist in the act of deterrence for the sake of changing conditions that result in violence would simply affirm that deterrence is motivated by mutual fear that allows the persistence of an 'us vs them' attitude to prevail. This attitude would further move some nations to prevent other nations from developing similar weapons of destruction (nuclear bombs) for fear that the latter may indiscriminately use such a destructive weapon. At the same time, other nations may simply persist with the production of weapons for destruction because they fear the threat of being annihilated. Results like this only confirm that the more things change, the more they remain the same. (The French Proverb: *Plus ça change, plus c'est la même chose.*) The more A persists to change B – while A remains the same – the more B persists in her/his behaviour to resist change because of the perceived threat of A's persistence. But what is really at stake in allowing this mental attitude, of 'us vs them' – an attitude that disconnects, separates, and divides – to prevail?

In this recursive relationship, each side of the conflict projects and assigns responsibility to the other as justification for what each is doing. In claiming that their voice was absolutely the 'right voice', and by implication that other voices were absolutely wrong, each punctuated their relationship as lineal or unilateral to justify their actions. In the micro relationship of persons in the personal story offered at the beginning of this Element, this is akin to A saying to B: 'If you simply change your opinion (believe that you are wrong), while I remain the same with my opinion (believe that I am right), our experience would be so much better'. In this instance, perhaps any relationship would be so much easier if there wasn't another person involved. But then again, it would also be meaningless. By definition relationships involve more than one and as such they can be maddening, frustrating, messy, and at the same time, exhilarating and too beautiful for words. In standing firm on their opinion of right and wrong, the experience of those in the personal story was such that it led to an impasse and feeling disconnected, frustrated, and angry.

What, however, is concealed in this persistence of 'who is right?' or 'who is wrong?' and claiming that only one of them can 'be right'? Allow me to share a story narrated by a systems thinker, von Foerster (1990), in his *Opening Address for the International Conference, Systems and Family Therapy: Ethics, Epistemology, New Methods.*

> I have a dear friend who grew up in Marrakech. The house of his family stood on the street that divide the Jewish and the Arabic quarter. As a boy he played with all the others, listened to what they thought and said, and learned of their fundamentally different views. When I asked him once, 'Who was right? he said, 'They are both right.' 'But this cannot be' I argued . . . 'Only one of them can have the truth!'
>
> 'The problem is not truth,' he answered, 'The problem is trust.'

This boy who lived on a street that divided the Jewish and Arabic quarter, remained connected to both Jews and Arabs by playing with them, listening to what each thought and had to say, and learning their fundamentally different views, and in so doing affirmed that the real problem is not one of who is right and who is wrong, but rather that it resided in the capacity to think and act in ways that offers a third (or fourth or fifth?) alternative. The quest for knowing 'who is right?' and 'who is wrong?' *closes-off alternatives.* It orients more to the disconnectedness among people rather that how they are connected. It socially divides those who live on a street that physically divides. But then again, can any street divide? Streets are simply there. Streets are constructed to make our travels easier. The boy in von Foerster's story affirms that the construction of any street offers the possibility of gathering persons who happen to live on either side of the street. Unlike the boy who chose to dwell by moving across both sides of the street, there was no intermingling of Jews and Arabs living on both sides of that street. 'Division' then is more a matter of how they chose to live on a street that was constructed. Within the context of violence and counter-violence, Lederach (2017) noted: 'Paradoxically they live as neighbours and yet are locked into long-standing cycles of hostile interaction' (p. 23). In the context of von Foerster's story, it is also a matter of long-standing cycles of 'no interaction'.

Growing out of this socially constructed division, the singular quest for *the* truth closes-off an understanding that what is really at stake is that they are both right. To accept that they are both right is to accept that both sides have *a* truth that not only needs to be heard and respected, but also that all voices need to feel heard. Without the everyday experience of playing together, talking, listening, and feeling heard, trust will not be a possibility. One emerging truth in the boy's response is that 'right or wrong' debates and disconnectedness deletes the possibility for trust to emerge in such a dualistically separated relationship. By implication, it also excludes the possibility to hope for and imagine a different relationship.

One natural outcome of dwelling in peace by preventing violence, and by remaining distrustful of the other, is, as noted earlier, the building of weapons of destruction – another expression of deterrence. Historically, the building of weapons of destruction led first to an Arms Race, and second, it also brought us into a realm of what was described as the 'cold war' between two 'superpowers, United States and the Soviet Union. Based on the ideological and geopolitical struggle for world dominance by these two superpowers, the Cold War ended with the collapse of the Soviet Union. But more than a struggle for dominance, Merton (2007), from within the confines of his monastery, noted that '"cold war" is simply the normal consequence of our corrupt idea of peace based on a policy of "every man for himself," in ethics, economics, and political like' (p. 122). There is *a* truth to Merton's assessment that it 'is absurd to hope for a solid peace based on mutual fear and a policy of every man or woman for themselves' (p. 122). In this, we are returned to Hobbes' 1651/1977) *Leviathan* way of living in mutual fear and that the best we can do is to hold on to building more armaments of destruction in order to feel secure.

To frame the problem of peace dwelling as a problem of trust and as a problem of increasing choices is to challenge a predominant and deeply ingrained dualistic either-or and right-wrong mental models. Determining who is right or who is wrong, would be a naturally forced consequence of this deeply ingrained either-or way of thinking. It is to think and act as if there are no, and can be no, other choices other than 'only one of them can have the truth'. Either-or thinking forces us to take sides (as if there are no other options). For Lederach (2005), who 'spent most of (his) professional life working with deep-rooted conflicts and violence' (p. 66), in this either-or model, 'side-taking, unfortunately seems to accompany social battlefields and therefore accepts the premise that change is inherently a dualistic struggle' (p. 87). Theoretically and practically, either-or thinking and doing, simply cannot resolve conflicts. On the contrary, they can only escalate conflicts.

To say that trust is what is at stake is to affirm that that how we choose to dwell or live together is that which is calling for our attention. Trust is essentially rooted in human association – in relationships. Trust is hard to define but can be felt inwardly and outwardly when it is present. Trust does not dwell in the opinionizing of opinions. The boy, in von Foerster's story, dwelt by remaining connected to both Jews and Arabs. He was able to dwell in trust because he chose to live in ways that nurtured and built trust. He did not build trust in order to dwell in peace. Instead, it was because of the way he dwelt that he allowed for the emergence of trust. It is this shift from thinking about peace as preventing violence to peace as residing or dwelling in ways that build trust, that informs another understanding of peace, namely, as cooperating for a growth of a culture of peace. And is not 'culture' also a matter of human association?

3.2 Peace as Cooperating for a Culture of Peace

On August 1, 1989, the Yamoussoukro declaration of 'Peace in the Minds of Men', which UNESCO adopted unanimously and by acclamation, changed UNESCO's 1945 thinking about peace. This 1989 declaration was divided into two interrelated and interconnected parts. First, it emphasized that peace is more than preventing violence, and expanded an understanding of peace as cooperating in ways that respects the primacy of the rule of law, pluralism, justice in international trade, and participation of the whole society. Second, they called for a growth of a culture of peace by showing a deep commitment to universal values of respect for life, freedom, justice, solidarity, tolerance, human rights, equality between women and men, and a harmonious partnership of humankind with the environment. Both of these interconnected parts were viewed as 'being the most precious possession of humanity' (UNESCO, n.d., p. 73), and as a way of promoting 'a healthy exercise of cooperation' (para 5).

Cooperation which respects the primacy of the rule of law (assuming that established laws are indeed good for all – recall, for example the Apartheid law of South Africa; Jim Crow laws in the United States that justified racial segregation; Taliban declaring jihad on women's rights), and showing a deep commitment to the identified values, including a harmonious partnership with the environment, are now placed under a rubric called a culture of peace. While we cannot deny the lived experience that it takes much 'cooperation' to fight a war in that each side must cooperate with the other to be an enemy, cooperation for peace appears to be much more difficult. The significance of approaching peace from the perspective of cooperating for a culture of peace is that it creates a public space for orienting to peace as being in the province of more than politicians and soldiers to include ALL. To speak of promoting a culture of peace is to focus on basic everyday actions like how we speak to each other, how we receive each other, how we listen to each other, how we play with each other, and *how we care for each other*. Culture, in this sense, includes and goes beyond appreciating the different foods we eat, or observing how people dance differently, or celebrating diverse customs. Instead, it is fundamentally a question of how we choose to dwell with each other and with our environment. In this way, culture is expressed through the spirited (animated) and soulful (spiritual) character of people who choose to dwell by connecting with each other despite their differences. Allow me to turn to Heidegger (1977) again and learn from what he said about dwelling and peace.

Heidegger (1977) informs us that we cannot talk about dwelling without talking about what we have built – with a twist. For him, building is really dwelling. 'We do not dwell,' he noted, 'because we have built, but we build and have built because we dwell, that is, because we are *dwellers*' (1977, p. 326; emphasis original). In this we can anticipate his distinction between peace building and peace dwelling. Heidegger returns us to the primal language of 'dwelling'.

> To be a human being means to dwell on earth as a mortal. It means to dwell. The old word *bauen* which says that man *is* insofar as he *dwells* ... also means ... to cherish, and protect, to preserve and care for ... The old Saxon *wuon*, the Gothic *wunian* ... means to remain, to stay in a place. But the Gothic *wunian* says more distinctly how this remaining is experienced. *Wunian* means to be at

peace, to be brought to peace, to remain in peace. The word for peace, *Friede*, means the free, *das Frye*; and *frye* means preserved from harm and danger, preserved from something, safeguarded. To free actually means to spare . . . To dwell, to be set at peace, means to remain at peace within the free . . . (Heidegger, 1977, p. 324, p. 326; emphasis original)

3.3 Being a Guardian

Notice, for instance that Heidegger speaks to how dwelling in peace, and remaining in peace is experienced. He formulated peace dwelling as being brought to peace and remaining at peace by caring for, sparing and safeguarding each other from harm and danger. These values and actions are collected under the rubric of being a Guardian. As guardians, peace dwellers spare each other from harm and thereby free all to be-at-home. For Heidegger (1977), the '*fundamental character of dwelling is this sparing*' (p. 327; emphasis original). It is particularly important to keep this character of dwelling in focus because in the literature on peace and conflict, the language of peace building and peace making, rather than peace dwelling, appears to dominate our consciousness (Lederach, 2005; Leonardsson and Rudd, 2015). As noted earlier, peace building is often addressed as an instrumental or technical means to an end. We build and re-build structures, systems, policies, and so forth, *in order to* live in peace. After violence or acts of war, peace builders engage in processes of reconciliation *in order to* repair past violations. Without disavowing the need to rebuild conditions for peace under those circumstances, Heidegger shifts our attention from this technical and instrumental relationship to peace building or peacemaking.

As a dweller, the boy in von Foerster's story remained in peace from the perspective of how he chose to dwell in a particular place. He chose to dwell by being clear about his place in-between the Arabic and Jewish quarters. In this his head and heart were 'straight', that is, not complicated. It was as if this boy demonstrated his maturity *both* by claiming his own voice *and* by enabling others to claim their own voices. Said differently, he was not a 'card-carrying' member of the Jews or Arabs in his dwelling place. It is as if this boy understood the philosopher Heidegger (1977), who noted that peace dwelling is experienced as 'being at peace', 'remaining at peace', or 'being brought to peace' by dwellers who *purposefully coordinate their efforts* to their dwelling in ways that cares, preserves, spares, and safeguards each other from harm and danger. His actions affirmed that he was indeed a guardian of those values. Guardianship defined his way of being. Rooted in the value of guardianship, this boy made an intentional and enlightened choice to dwell in ways that cared for all in his own back yard. He did not do anything extraordinary. He did ordinary things. He played with all, he listened to all, and he sought to understand what was important to both Arabs and Jews. In doing ordinary things, he can, however, be viewed as doing extraordinary things (crazy things?), because he chose to step out of the boundaries of how Arabs and Jews chose to ordinarily live on that street.

In the extraordinariness of his ordinariness, he exemplified what being a dweller means. Listening to Heidegger, we can say that this boy's enlightened choice is a call for all who live on any street to gather together by taking responsibility to embrace and embody the principle of Guardianship. And how is this done? By subordinating or surrendering themselves to being governed by the principles of caring, preserving, sparing, and safeguarding each other from harm and danger. Why? Because this is what dwellers as Guardians value and do. As Guardians, dwellers act in ways that are aware of how their actions would affect, and indeed, cannot not affect every other group or person.

3.4 Peace as *Shalom*

This understanding of dwellers as Guardians is closely connected to the biblical and Judaic concept of *shalom*. From the perspective of the World Churches Council (2012), *shalom* focuses 'on justice, prosperity, and wholeness' (p. 26). *Shalom* calls all persons to care for the well-being of the whole and for the prosperity and justice for all. This is *Shalom*'s culture of peace.

In this, we are retuned to Kornfield's (1993) notion of 'true community'. As mentioned earlier in this Element, true community 'arises when we can speak in accord with truth and compassion', when we 'come together bringing honesty, respect, and kindness to support an awakening of the sacred' (p. 24). In this way, *shalom* genuinely embraces and embodies the values of honesty, respect, truth, compassion, justice, and kindness, to support an awakening of the sacred. Sacred in the sense that the Guardianship of principles of caring preserving, sparing, and safeguarding each other from harm and danger are non-negotiable and indispensable should we choose to work towards being a true community, or, as Kornfield (1993) would say, a 'spiritual community'. Insofar as *Shalom* focuses on justice, prosperity, and wholeness, it is indeed revealing to see Aristotle (1962) as raising the question: 'How could prosperity be safeguarded and preserved without friends?' (Line 1155a, p. 10). The concept of *shalom* is now moving us to consider peace and peace dwelling from the perspective of friendship.

3.5 Peace as Friendship

In Book VIII of his *Nichomachean Ethics*, Aristotle (1962) offered us a 'practical' understanding of friendship through his observation of the practices of politicians and lawgivers during his time:

> Friendship . . . seems to hold states together, and lawgivers apparently devote more attention to it than to justice. For concord seems to be something similar to friendship, and concord is what they most strive to attain, while they do their best to expel faction, the enemy of discord. When people are friends, they have no need for justice, but when they are just, they need friendship in addition. In fact, the just, in the fullest sense is regarded as constituting an element of friendship. (Aristotle, 1962, Line 1155a, pp. 23–29)

Friendship, according to Aristotle, was the lawgivers' way of striving to attain concord and harmony. They paid more attention to friendship than to justice in the traditional legalistic sense of justice. What is unique and significant in Aristotle's formulation of friendship is the notion that when 'people are friends, they have no need for justice, but when they are just, they need friendship in addition . . .' (Aristotle, 1962, 1155a, p. 29). Could this be his way of challenging Plato's claim that the *Republic* be rooted in justice?

In terms of peace as friendship and from the point of view of caring for justice, prosperity, and wholeness (*shalom*), in Canada's relationship with its Indigenous people, for example, we hear an Indigenous author Ladner (2009) as pointing to the limits of Canada's legalistic structure: 'Given that the courts have been . . . quite useless as an arena in which [Canada's] constitutional orders can be reconciled,' she opined, 'some alternative mechanisms need to be developed' (p. 296). Perhaps the alternative of friendship is indeed what is at stake for holding Canadians together as 'we are all here to stay' (Ladner, 2009, p. 287).

It is here that we need to uncover Aristotle's distinction between three kinds of friendship, and to be aware of the reciprocity of motives underpinning each of these kinds of friendships (Aristotle, 1962, Line 1155b, p. 31).

> when the motive . . . is usefulness, the partners do not feel affection for one another *per se* but in terms of the good accruing to each from the other. The same is also true of those whose friendship is based on pleasure: we love witty people not for what they are, but for the pleasure they give us. (Aristotle, 1962, Line 1156a, pp. 10–13)

In both of these motives of usefulness and pleasure, the other 'is loved not because he [she] is a friend, but because he [she] is useful or pleasant' (Aristotle, 1962, Line 1156a, p. 15). In the literature on leadership studies, we notice that both these kinds of relationships are defined under a rubric called transactional leadership. In this relationship, transactional leaders exchange things of what is regarded as valuable to both leaders and followers in order to advance their own and their followers' agendas (Kuhnert, 1994). In this mode of exchange, followers do what leaders want them to do because it is in their best interests to do so (Kuhnert and Lewis, 1987). This transaction or exchange involves something that is regarded as valuable between what the leader possesses or controls and what followers wants in return for their services (Yukl and Van Fleet 1992). A challenge and reality of transactional relationships is that the 'affection' felt between leaders and followers are at best ephemeral and temporary. In cases like this, both leaders and the followers are motivated to ask: 'What's in it for me to remain in this relationship?' Simply put, when the relationship is no longer experienced as benefitting one or the other, that relationship is simply altered into uselessness or as being unpleasant.

Aristotle (1962) offered a third kind of friendship, which he called 'the perfect form of friendship', namely, 'those who wish for their friends' good, for their friends' sake . . .' and which for him, 'are friends in the truest sense' (Aristotle, 1962, Line 1156b, p. 10). It is in this way that we can also understand Pope Pius VI's (1972) notion of peace. In his *Message for the Celebration of the Day of Peace* (Jan. 1, 1972), he stated: 'If you want peace, work for justice.' And he went on to locate the 'true source' of peace, as being 'rooted in a sincere feeling for man . . . And what do we call this sincere feeling for man? We call it Justice' (Pope Pius VI, 1972, para 5 & 6). This form of friendship and justice is not based on motives of transactional affection. Instead, it is a sincere feeling that 'is determined by what their friends are and not by incidental considerations' (Aristotle, 1962, Line 1156b, p. 10). The etymology of the word sincerity may add to the genuineness of such a feeling. Sincerity is composed of two Latin words: *sine* (meaning *without*) and *cera* (meaning *wax*). The genuineness of a sincere feeling for others is such that it is 'without wax'.

For Aristotle (1962), however, friendship is more than simply wishing the best for the other. In this Aristotle is clear: 'One cannot extend friendship to or be a friend of another person until each partner has impressed the other that he is worthy of affection, and until each has won the other's confidence' (Aristotle, 1962, Line 1156b, p. 30). In quoting a proverb, he shared that people cannot become worthy of each other's affection 'until they have eaten the specified (measure of salt) together' (Aristotle, 1962, Line 1156b, p. 25; parenthesis original). It is in this reciprocal interaction of being guided by the principle of friendship, namely by giving and receiving the best of what we can give and receive from the other, *and vice versa*, by experiencing the pains (eating the specified measure of salt together) and the joys of winning the other's confidence, that true friendship emerges in its fullness. Living together in friendship then is both a sincere feeling and an act. Without wax, it is a feeling that wishes the best for the other, a feeling that seeks not to prevail over the other, and it is a decision to act deliberately in ways that are influenced by such a feeling for their friend's sake. In this process people *become* friends by gaining each other's confidence. The reciprocity of this relationship affirms that 'friends should be able to count on' each person receiving in all matters what he gives the other

(Aristotle, 1962, Line 1156b, p. 35). It is in this relationship of friendliness that we can begin to understand Aristotle when he said: 'When people are friends, they have no need for justice, but when they are just, they need friendship in addition' (Aristotle, 1962, Line 1155a, p. 28).

4 Peace Leadership as an Affair of the Heart: On Being a Curator

Thus far, we see that caring for the spirit and souls of individuals and the community, cooperating for a culture of peace by caring preserving, sparing, and safeguarding each other from harm and danger, shalom, and friendship, emerge as critical human values for dwelling in peace. These values are collected under the concept and principle of Guardianship – peace dwellers are guardians. The complexity of embodying Guardianship within the context of violence that we witness in our world today is such that we find ourselves in the middle of betrayal, distrust, and dehumanizing practices that stand in the way of dwelling in peace and remaining at peace. Violence, counter-violence, and mutual fear that the other does not have the other's best interests at heart, affirm that we find ourselves in the middle of a brokenness of trust and as if we have no options other than either/or – right/wrong.

In this context, we turn our attention to Burns' (1978) second fundamental act of leadership, namely 'to induce people to be aware or conscious of what they feel, to feel their needs so strongly, to define their values so meaningfully . . .' (p. 44). From the preceding paragraph, the need to be aware and conscious of being a guardian, surfaces as a critical value for peace dwellers. But why induce anyone to be aware or conscious of and feel the need to be a Guardian? Because, as Burns (1978) quotes Susanne Langer, 'where nothing is felt, nothing matters'. If, as Gadamer (1996c) noted, 'practice' (of 'being aware or conscious of what they feel') 'always has a relationship to a person's being' (pp. 3–4), then it appears as if Burns (1978, 2003) has taken a page out of the wisdom of old books. For example, Confucius, the Latin name for Kong Fuzi, who lived around 500 BCE already laid down a path for those who seek to put a disorderly (violent) world in order:

> To put the world in order, we must put the nation in order,
> To put the nation in order, we must put the family in order,
> To put the family in order, we must first cultivate our personal life,
> And to cultivate our personal life, we must first set our hearts straight.
> (as cited in Estes, 2017, p. 10)

Kong Fuzi's thinking has filtered itself through the centuries. Speaking from a Christian perspective, Merton for example, added a spiritual component: 'We are not at peace with others because we are not at peace with ourselves, and we are not at peace with ourselves because we are not at peace with God' (as cited in Givey, 2009, p. xvii). And in his book *New Seeds of Contemplation*, Merton (2007) went on to say:

> So instead of loving what you think is peace, love other men and love God above all. And instead of hating the people you think are warmakers, hate the appetites and disorder in your own soul, which are the causes of war. If you love peace, then hate injustice, the tyranny, hate greed, but hate these things *in yourself*, not in another. (Merton, 2007, p. 122; emphasis in original)

The intrapersonal quest to set our *hearts* straight (Kong Fuzi) and to search for the disorder in one's *soul* (Merton) are ways of dwelling in peace with ourselves and with something other than ourselves – God. In our world of deep division, Moore (2009) joins Merton is saying that what we need is 'soul … holding together mind and body, ideas and life, spirituality and the world' (p. xiv). Within Christianity for example, priests in their parishes are called to accept the responsibility and the work known as *cura animarum*, which means Curators who care for the souls of their parishioners. Similarly, Moore (1992) suggested that we can also be 'the curates or curators of our own souls' (p. xv) and for Kong Fuzi, it means that we can also be Curators of our own hearts.

How then can peace dwellers – as Guardians – go about the task of inducing dwellers to feel the need to be Curators of their souls and hearts as they themselves experience the disturbance of the brokenness of trust? If this value of being a Curator is not embodied in everyday life, and if an individual or a collective is immersed in only feeling the effects of betrayal (e.g. remaining angry, doubtful; distrustful), or for that matter engrossed in orienting to others only as enemies, it could as Galtung (2001) argued, generate a 'meta conflict', namely a 'conflict that comes out of, or after the root conflict, the over layer' (p. 3). For Lumsden (1999) this traumatic meta-conflict can become an '*unconscious organizing principle*' (p. 3, emphasis original), in that it can determine how people see the world a generation later and how they choose to act. This unconscious organizing principle can perpetuate killing the other or legitimizing other violent forms of dealing with conflict.

4.1 Feeling Disturbed

Allow me to turn my attention to the question raised in the previous paragraph by returning to the 'incident' for this Element. While participants in that workshop came together or gathered because they were interested in responding to the question of how they care for themselves and for each other while living in the gap between their aspirations (peace) and what is (violence), they also gathered within the context of being disturbed by what they were seeing in the Middle East. The good news about feeling disturbed is that they were not feeling indifferent. In this process, what bubbled up in being disturbed were feelings of anger, resentment, and frustration. In that emotional state of restlessness (being-not-at-home) while they noisily accused each other of not understanding ('No, No, No, You Don't Understand'), they all shared in feeling the injustice of what they were witnessing in the Middle East. They were not then angry with each other, but angry at the experience of injustice – as they saw it. What they essentially cared about was people suffering an injustice. This is what mattered most to them, and they each wanted their voice to be heard.

However, for the sake of feeling heard, while the Peace Prayer of St. Francis urges us to seek first to understand and then to be understood, in this room, the reverse held to be true. In the desperate desire to be heard, their loud voices drowned the possibility of listening. Allow me to use the language of 'I'. As a peace facilitator, I intuited that underlying their anger was their experience of being hurt. They were each disturbed and hurting from what they saw taking place in public. And as a facilitator, I acted on my intuition. There was no time or inclination to do an empirical survey to validate what I sensed. I needed to trust my own senses/intuitions. Even though I, as their facilitator, was charged with being 'crazy', it appeared as an appropriate thing to do in <u>that</u> circumstance.

4.2 Curators Embrace Compassion and Healing

In embodying the spirit of a Curator, the peculiar character of judging the appropriateness of an act based on 'intuition' is difficult to define. Perhaps such a character resists definition. At a personal level, what I do know and want to acknowledge is that such an 'intuition' was itself a consequence of me, as facilitator, asking the Lord for help. Could this then be conceptualized as a moment of grace? In Genesis 6:8, grace is described as 'God's favour'. If this is true, then this gift of intuition can be received as a favour that was freely given by the Divine. This is indeed humbling because it affirms that human beings are but conduits of a something larger than themselves and all we need to do is to be open to the possibility of being surprised. It times of hurt, Curators understand that *compassion* is a more appropriate response. This is what Curators hold true. The etymology of the word 'compassion' can help us better understand what it means to be a curator. The word 'compassion' is composed of two Latin words: *com* (with or together) and *pati* which means *to suffer*. Compassion means 'to suffer together'. To respond with compassion, then, is to look for proper and appropriate ways to 'suffer together' for the sake of 'healing'. It is in this way that Curators choose to be a healing presence. Curators then are not focused on 'curing' restlessness but rather on 'healing' the restlessness of being-not-at-home.

The significance of the practice of healing is that unlike notions of building and making, it does not 'produce' anything. Musicians, for example, may create or produce beautiful pieces of music. Artists way produce paintings never before painted. Poets may produce poetry that touches the core of our hearts. While these may be shared with others, their products remain theirs. Those are their possessions. Unlike them, Curators cannot be seen as producing anything. Nothing tangible is left behind. Such is the nature of healing. Within the context of disturbance, healing aims at restoring broken relationships to once again becoming whole. According to Gadamer (1996c):

> The expert practice of this art [healing] inserts itself entirely within the process of nature in so far as it seeks to restore this process when it is disturbed, and to do so in such a way that the art can allow itself to disappear once the natural equilibrium of health has returned. (p. 34)

Within the context of the 'incident', the silence of participants, after they joined-in in singing and humming to St. Francis' Peace Prayer, and hugging each other with their hands, could be interpreted as them choosing to return themselves to a state of equilibrium.

4.3 Another Personal Story

Allow me to describe this experience of reclaiming equilibrium (or not) through my passion for cycling. Yes, I have been riding my bicycle ever since I was a very young boy. The bicycle was my main mode of transportation, in my hometown, Taiping, in Malaysia. Curiously, Taiping means 'eternal peace'. My first experience of riding a bicycle was one of being totally off-balanced. I found myself leaning too much to the left, and in an effort to stay balanced I leaned too much to the right. The result: I crashed. Falling and crashing were not a matter of applying no force or applying little force to stay balanced, but rather a matter of applying too much force. After several attempts suddenly everything appeared to happen spontaneously, lightly, and effortlessly. After a while, I was able to boast riding my bicycle with arms folded: 'Look Ma, no hands'. And then, my arrogance got the better of me. I decided to experiment riding my bicycle with my left hand on the right handle, and my right hand on the left handle. I crashed. As I was falling, in my panic-stricken state, instead of letting go, I held on to the handles more tightly, and against rational thinking – I began to ride faster. Result: I broke my right hand, dislocated the other, and had bruises in my legs. My bike was in a sorry state. I limped home with bike in tow. It was an experiment that failed miserably. The best I received from my mom after I told her what I did, was: 'You idiot!' And she was right. Today, I enjoy riding my bike with right hand on right handle and left hand on left handle.

What is the point of this story? In times of social disturbance, reclaiming a state of equilibrium or harmony, cannot be a matter of applying too much force, and neither can it be a matter of ignoring some basic 'rules'. Metaphorically, keeping left hand on left handle and right hand on right handle is critical to discerning what is being called for in moments of disturbance. The challenge, however, is that in times of violence, decisions to stay balanced are being made in a panic-stricken state. Consequently, there is a real need to slow down, take one's hands 'off the handles' of our thoughts for vengeance or counter-violence, and to take a step back, for the sake of discerning what it means to be a healing presence. Failure to do so might only invite my mother's admonition 'You Idiot!' In the example of the 'incident', and in retrospect, for the sake of healing – a gentle and seemingly 'crazy' (unexpected/risky) response of singing may not only be the precise pressure or force that is required to reclaim a state of equilibrium and harmony, but it can also be a way of reconstructing conditions for being-at-home.

4.4 A Change in Focus

It is here that we need to take another look at Heidegger's (1977) formulation of what *proper gathering* means: 'It is proper to every gathering that gatherers assemble to coordinate their efforts to sheltering; only when they have gathered with that end in mind, do they begin to gather' (n.p.). What is particularly relevant here is a subtle, yet significant, shift, and its implications for dwelling in peace. At the risk of repetition, dwelling in peace is not so much a matter of resolving the conflict or conflicted feelings of participants in that incident. It is not a matter of coming to any kind of consensus. It is not a problem to be solved. Instead, it is a matter of leaning into the problem of living decisively in the messiness of this in-between space of peace and violence/disturbance, by coordinating our efforts and paying attention to how we choose to shelter or dwell in the context of what is being presented to us in our Here and Now. It is precisely because we know that how we choose to interact with each other in our Here and Now will influence the relationships that we build for ourselves inside and outside of any shared space, that it is both necessary and desirable that peace leaders as Curators need to keep this (namely, *coordinating efforts to sheltering*) as the end in mind.

If compassion and healing is truly what is at stake, then it would be foolish to give into the temptation of engaging in any *discussion* about who is right or who is wrong. By its own etymology, dis-cussion as *dis* (meaning *apart*) and *cutere* (meaning *to cut*), will lead each speaker to *cut the other off* or *cut apart* what the other has to say. In the presence and context of persons who are hurting, it is not more discussion that is needed. Within the context of the 'incident' presented, for the sake of inducing persons to be conscious of feeling the need for compassion and healing, peace leaders as Curators would need to take a step back, step out of circles of acrimony, imagine and risk constructing a healing space within any publicly constructed conversational spaces by raising and acting on the question of what it means to dwell and how we need to dwell with each other in times of acrimony. If we accept this, then Curators are called to properly coordinate the efforts of all who are restless to shelter and dwell in ways that are healing.

For Heidegger (1977), this dimension of dwelling makes a particular demand on us: 'The proper dwelling plight lies in this, that mortals ever search anew for the essence of dwelling, that they must *ever learn to dwell*' (p. 363; emphasis original). Continuous learning (ever learn) is a critical term for Heidegger. Within the context of the personal story, the learning that is proper for this gathering is to attend to the particularities of what is being asked for *in that situation* or *context.* It cannot be abstract. The etymology of the word 'abstract' can be understood from the Latin *abstrahere*, meaning *to draw away from*, or *ab-stare* meaning to stand away from. Peace leaders as Curators cannot draw their attention away from or stand apart from the particularity of their situation or context because particular situations raise particular questions, and they demand particular answers. And so, learning to dwell in peace within the context of the personal story, involves continuously attending to the details of not only how participants in that story chose to inhabit or dwell in that space but also how they could dwell. It also needs to include how peace leaders as Curators choose to dwell in moments that appear acrimonious and in moments that are defined by the predictability of unpredictability. In defining that situation as persons feeling hurt, such a definition could potentially open peace leaders to being governed by the value of being a Curator which in turn orients them to healing and being a healing presence.

What, however, would it mean to <u>not</u> attend to being a Curator? Hurts run deep. Hurts are painful. They can take up their place and solidify or harden in the depths of one's heart and soul. In so doing, one's heart of flesh can become a heart of stone. In relation to the continual conflict in the Middle East; we can see the hardened and hurting hearts playing itself out in public- violently. The injustice of structural elements in that society continues to feed the hardening of hearts and the hurt. The betrayal and absence of trust sustains hearts of stone. Ill-will prevails. Here there are no friends. Only enemies. But here's the thing. Because hurt runs deep, hurt is not readily visible. The overlayer, anger and angry reactions, is more visible and it presents itself directly for others to see. Reverting to the personal story (incident), what we see is that participants were angry on the outside but hurting on the inside. Talking over each other is an expression of such anger. The fixation and the fixing of hearts that appeared like stones are readily exposed as anger and resentment. We do not readily see – what is concealed – is that they are hurting on the inside. Perhaps this is why prophet Ezekiel from the Old Testament, spoke to the need to transform hearts of stone to hearts of flesh.

> for the sake of my holy name which you have profaned ... I shall give you a new heart and put a new spirit in you. I shall remove the heart of stone in your bodies and give you a heart of flesh instead. (Ezekiel, 36:23–26)

For the prophet Ezekiel the transforming of hearts of stone to hearts of flesh is necessary for the sake of something *other*. For him, such a spiritual transformation is desirable for the sake of His holy name. Could we also not say, that for the sake of the holiness of peace, which has been profaned and defiled through the hardening of hearts, we need to 'remove' our hearts of stone and welcome hearts of flesh for the sake of something '*other*' that is not readily visible? Is this not what Burns (2003) meant by transforming leadership?

> to transform something cuts much more profoundly. It is to cause a metamorphosis in form or structure, a change in the very condition or nature of a thing, a change into another substance, a radical change in outward form or inner character ... It is change of this breadth and depth that is fostered by transforming leadership. (Burns, 2003, p. 24)

For Burns (2003) radical change in outward form and inner character is the purpose of transforming leadership. This radical transforming change is also echoed by O'Dea (2012), a renowned figure in international social healing and peace studies. For him, an ambassador of peace 'recognizes the importance of transforming both inner blockages to peace and those blockages in external relations, cultures, and systems that prevent peace in the world' (O'Dea, 2012, p. ii). He would further say that as 'fluently' as peace ambassadors 'model and express peace', they must also 'learn to reflect and embody it' (O'Dea, 2012, p. ii). For Burns (2003), one significant way that peace leaders can model, and express leadership is by partnering with the dispossessed of the world and by empowering both leaders and followers with a transforming purpose. For him such a modelling and expressing is 'the greatest moral undertaking of united leadership' (Burns, 2003, p. 3).

4.5 Embodying a Sacred Heart

For Heifetz and Linsky (2017), such a modelling would mean choosing to lead and dwell with an open and 'sacred heart'. 'The virtue of a sacred heart', they said, 'lies in the courage to maintain your innocence and wonder, your doubt and curiosity . . . your compassion and love even through moments of despair' (p. 227). Embodying a 'sacred heart' means that while Curators 'may feel tortured and betrayed, powerless and hopeless', they can choose to 'stay open . . . without hardening or closing [themselves]' (pp. 229–230). The power of the sacred heart is such that 'even in the midst of disappointment and defeat', Curators can 'still remain connected to people and to the source of your most profound purposes' (p. 230). How then can peace leaders as Curators attend to the work of transforming hearts of stone to hearts of flesh? How can they go about the process of inducing the need to feel the need to be a Curator of their hearts and souls in moments of disturbance? I offer three Curator 'practices': song, stories/story telling, and poetry.

4.6 Song

One practical, meaningful, and improvisational method could be the use of song. Not any song, but songs and music that are particularly connected to the experience at hand. So, this procedure itself would depend on a person's knowledge of a number of different songs and their openness and courage to use them spontaneously. Stephen Holley, coordinator of the Commercial Music Program at the Kent Denver School in Englewood, Colorado, for example, shared his story that 'a musician has the responsibility to listen, react, adjust, refocus, and add to the conversation on an almost constant basis!' 'This', he continues to say, 'is true in all styles of music but is arguably most prevalent in jazz and other improvisational genres' (as cited in Webb, 2011, Para 2). But more than being responsibly engaged in a conversation, for film composer Bernard Hermann, music can also 'propel narrative swiftly forward, or slow it down. It often lifts mere dialogue into the realm of poetry' (as cited in Wentz, 2013, Para 1). This is Hermann's story. For him the power of improvisational music lies in its capacity to lift mere talk into the realm of poetry. Similarly, the lived experience of the personal story shared in this Element, affirms that song can move people in powerful ways. It can inspire, draw emotional responses like crying, compel us to remain calm and silent, and allow for healing.

Within the context of the personal story, the Peace Prayer of St. Francis appeared to be an appropriate song. The singing and humming of that song was not planned. Indeed, it was spontaneous. In retrospect, the spontaneity of singing and humming to that song/hymn is experienced as a divine gift and an affirmation that this aspect of knowing cannot be a matter of planning, or control. For Gadamer (1996d), spontaneity and subsequent improvisational

Curator practices, places us in 'the so-called grey areas where things cannot be treated with scientific exactitude' (p. 133). As a facilitator, my lived experience was such that I appealed to the Good Lord for help, and I believe that the Prayer of St. Francis was His answer to my prayer. In retrospect, my lived experience also meant a knowing that to act on His answer was also a risk in that it would appear as if logic was being dismissed. Consequently, Curators may, as experienced in that personal story, be charged with 'crazy making'. This 'charge' however, presupposes that there is an objective standard and rules by which to judge this, or that act as not crazy.

In a situation of disharmony, shouting in order to be heard, and hammering things out in the heat of the moment (heated discussions), appeared to be accepted as not crazy-making ways of being. Expressing anger and resentment at the injustice of violence may be accepted as not crazy making, and by implication 'normal'. From the perspective of whatever is accepted as an objective and normal standard, singing or humming in a moment of disturbance on the other hand, may be viewed as avoiding the task of addressing and settling disharmony, let alone taking such a situation seriously. However, the lived experience in that situation was that the very methods and procedures of shouting, and hammering things out, were themselves dysfunctional in that these methods paradoxically precluded the attainment of harmony. It led instead to more disharmony. In this context, 'crazy-making' can only be viewed as an illogical solution to resolve logical problems. Singing in the middle of escalating accusations of not understanding ('No! No! No! You don't understand!') makes 'no sense' in that context – hence crazy, by definition and effect. A logical response to what seemed like crazy behaviour is confusion ('Some stared at me . . .'). Accusations of 'being crazy' can be interpreted as an attempt to regain a preconceived notion of 'normalcy' and in so doing, regain a sense of clarity (not confused).

Insofar as peace leaders as Curators intentionally and deliberately use song with the awareness that they maybe charged with crazy making (or not), this very awareness implies that they are not crazy but intentional (Amaladas, 2018). They are intentional in acting unpredictably in a world that favours the predictability of whatever is accepted as normal. They are deliberate in their awareness of the need to step out of established system of rules and relationships governing matters regarding how to dwell amid conditions of pain and suffering. They are also deliberate in their consciousness that they need to break cycles of action-reaction by moving away from a defined place of 'normalcy' to what maybe viewed as a 'strange' and 'crazy' place, with the imagination that all can be brought to peace in a newly re-defined place.

4.6.1 Risking Vulnerability

In their awareness that they are taking a risk in acting in crazy-making ways, Curators open themselves up to becoming vulnerable. And herein lies yet another paradox. The word vulnerability comes from the Latin *vulnus, vulnere,* which means *wound, to wound.* In creating conditions to meaningfully heal the wound-edness of others, Curators open themselves up to being wounded. This lived experience affirms what Arendt (1958) shared, namely, that 'because the actor always moves among and in relation to other acting beings, he is never merely a 'doer' but always and at the same time a sufferer' (p. 190). She goes on to say:

> To do and to suffer are like opposite sides of the same coin, and the story that an act starts is composed of its consequent deeds and sufferings. These consequences are boundless, because action, though it may proceed from nowhere ... acts into a medium where every reaction becomes a chain reaction, and where every process is the cause of new processes ... This boundlessness is characteristic not of political action alone ... the smallest act in the most limited circumstances bears the seed of the same boundlessness, because one deed, and sometimes one word, suffices to change every constellation. (p. 190)

The boundlessness of the lived experience of the personal story, in its most limited circumstances, and in particular the reaction to the act of singing and humming to Saint Francis' Prayer of Peace, evolved from reactions of disbelief and confusion ('staring ...'), to an accusation that their peace facilitator was simply dismissing the need to be serious ('are you crazy?'), to joining-in the facilitator's craziness of singing and humming to the Peace Prayer song/hymn, and ending with a moment of silence, and tears. Such was the outward and inward change experienced at that moment.

In accepting the risk of being wounded, that small act of orienting to a different script (singing/ humming to a different song), enabled a change that allowed blood and air to flow freely once again to a rejuvenated heart. The power in that one small deed is that it enabled an evolution from heated discussion and accusations to joining in the singing/humming, and to a silence that enabled each and every one of them to search their own hearts and to set their hearts straight. It was not a paralyzing silence. This one small and risky deed enabled the possibility of a radical change from hearts of stone to hearts of flesh. It was as if they experienced a warm embrace of coming-home. Therein was the surprise for all. On a personal note, did I, as their facilitator, know that this would be the outcome? No. Was such a deed worth it? In this instance, and only in retrospect – Yes. Therein lies *a* truth to the boundlessness of any act. We simply cannot predict the unpredictability of the consequences of our actions. The best that Curators can do in circumstances like this is to *hope* for the best because hope keeps the imagination and the possibility that things could be otherwise, alive.

4.7 Stories/Story Telling

This Element began with the telling a story of an incident at a particular point in time and context, and proceeded by telling a story about that story. As a psychologist Mair (1988) wrote:

> Stories are habitations. We live in and through stories. They conjure worlds. We do not know the world other than story world. Stories inform life. They hold us together and keep us apart. We inhabit the great stories of our culture. We live through stories. We are lived by the stories of our race and place. It is this enveloping and constituting function of stories that is especially import-ant to sense more fully. We are, each of us, locations where the stories of our place and time become partially tellable. (p. 127)

To accept that we live in and through the stories we tell is to accept that we both live the stories of our culture, race and place, and are lived by those stories. We dwell in our stories and our stories dwell in us. The strength of stories is such that we first make our stories and then our stories make us. The angry reactions of participants in that workshop, for example, were expressions of how they were living the stories that were telling themselves and how they were being lived by such a telling. For Mair (1988), this is precisely what is 'important to sense more fully' (p. 127). This sensing of stories goes beyond fictions and tales. It is the stuff of human experience, including our histories, politics, economics, sciences, and religions. Our human experience is a storied experience. Each and every one of us is not only a storyteller but we are also storied beings. Every theory, book, or conversation is an exercise in storytelling. The storying of Peace Dwelling in this Element is but a story. For Mair (1988) what is important to sense fully is our awareness of how the stories we tell ourselves and each other are living our lives for us. Being conscious of this frees us to understand that the stories we tell are but a story based on socialized preconceptions or categories within our worldviews. This awareness opens us up to the possibility of telling different stories. We become open to alternate stories by becoming aware that our stories are socially constructed on the basis of our socialized preconceptions and categories that are informed by culture, race, and place.

In relation to transformative change, Habermas (1984), a critical theorist, pointed to another revealing truth that is embedded in storytelling.

> When we tell stories we cannot avoid also saying indirectly how the subjects involved in them are faring and what fate the collectivity they belong is experiencing. Nevertheless, we can make harm to personal or threats to social integration visible only indirectly in narratives. (p. 137)

In telling a story about my personal story that participants in that workshop were experiencing the pain of hurt, and as naming how they were faring as hurting is to say that dwelling in peace draws peace leaders as Curators into the work of editing. They listen, edit, and reshape stories that are being told by how they listen, by the questions they ask, and by choosing to focus and elaborate on certain parts of the story. This is also true for all persons in any setting. Persons in that particular workshop were editing what they chose to hear or not hear. Such an editing can construct walls or destroy walls. And here, we may be well advised to hear the words of the poet Frost (1914), in his poem *Mending Wall*: 'Before I built a wall, I'd ask to know, What I was walling in or walling out, And to whom I was like to give offence' (Lines 32–33). The significance of this *edited listening* is that both Curators and participants can listen and act in ways other than what either of them intended – precisely because of such an editing. Curators, in other words, are not in control. This lived experience makes visible what Senge (2006), an organizational learning theorist, meant when he wrote:

> when we bring people together for a . . . conversation, the only thing I control is the construction of the space, and the construction of intention . . . The rest of it, I don't control. It is controlled by the people who are there through their conversations and interactions. (p. 330)

While the purposeful construction of conversational spaces and intentions may lie within the 'control' of Curators, 'the rest of it' it is in the hands, minds, and hearts of the collective. From this perspective it appears as if the best that peace leaders as Curators can do is *to initiate* conversations on peace. Without others 'joining-in' in ways that are aligned with what is intended, the experience within such socially constructed spaces can become messy.

Insofar as Burns (2003), suggested that 'leaders take the initiative in mobilizing people for participation in the process of change' (p. 25), the understanding of peace leadership as a relationship, means that the effectiveness in realizing the Curator's *initiative* is directly dependent upon the followers' voluntary willingness to 'join in'. Leadership, in other words, is embedded in the relationship between a leader's *initiative* and followers' voluntary and willing decision to 'join-in' (or not). For an existentialist philosopher, Buber (1970), it is a relationship that is established on the grounds of reciprocity. For him, any relationship other than reciprocity, 'dilutes the meaning of relations' (p. 58), or what it means to be in a relationship. At the same time, the language of 'initiative' alerts us to the question of what it means to act. Arendt's (1958) excellent unveiling of different meanings of what it means to act is worthy of a second look. The Greek and Latin languages, she sketched, contain two different, yet interrelated, words to designate the verb 'to act'. To the two Greek verbs, *archein* ('to begin', 'to lead', and finally 'to rule') and *prattein* ('to pass through', 'to achieve', 'to finish') correspond the two Latin verbs *agere* ('to set in motion', 'to lead') and *gerere* whose original meaning is 'to bear') (p. 189, parenthesis and emphasis in original).

Within our leadership literature, our consciousness has been dominated by an understanding of action as *archein* (begin) and *prattein* (finish). In the field of leadership studies, we encounter a dominant acceptance of how the effectiveness of leadership is to be 'measured'. For example, Burns (1978) described leadership effectiveness in the following way: 'the test of the extent and quality of power and leadership is the degree of actual accomplishment of the promised change' (p. 461). Elsewhere, Burns (2006) talked about leadership as 'the interaction of persons in human (and inhuman) conditions of equality – an interaction measured by ethical and moral values and by the degree of realization of intended, comprehensive, and desirable change' (p. 239). What has dropped out of sight in our leadership discourse is the notion of acting as beginning something new or to set in motion (*agere*), and the subsequent experiences of leaders and followers from within that frame of reference. What is critical to note in Arendt's (1958) very perceptive distinctions is that to think of leadership action as 'to set in motion' (*agere*) is to accept that 'the strength of the beginner shows itself only in his initiative and the risk he takes, not in the actual achievement' (p. 190). To initiate anything, to set something in motion, is to risk the unpredictability of finishing the intended task. It is precisely this understanding of action as initiative that allowed Rost (1991) to claim that 'leadership may still be leadership when the relationship fails to *produce* results' (p. 118; emphasis original). In saying this Rost (1991) joins Arendt (1958) who formulated the strength of the initiator as showing itself only in the initiative and the risks taken, and not in the actual achievement. Both Rost and Arendt then make a break from Burns (2003) who noted that the leadership 'test' is in 'the results' attained (p. 3).

In any *initiative* peace leaders find themselves alone. Others may join in or not; others may join-in and finish the task as intended, or not. While the courage to set something new in motion, and <u>strength</u> of any initiative belongs to the initiator, the <u>power</u> of any initiative belongs to the collective who may or may not choose to bear the burden (*gerere)* of joining-in and finishing (*prattein*) the initiator's task. In this, Curators as initiators are not in control. To this end, we can also understand how Rost's (1991) understanding of leadership effectiveness, as formulated through Arendt's (1958) distinction of *agere* and *gerere*, is connected to Weber's (1978) formulation of *value rational action*. As noted earlier, for Weber (1978), value rational action is 'determined by a conscious belief in the value for its own sake . . . <u>independently of its prospects for success</u>' (pp. 24–25; emphasis added). At the same time, the voluntary joining-in does not automatically mean that both leaders and followers will always be involved in initiatives aimed at the common good. Such relationships and initiatives can be toxic (Lipman-Blumen, 2006; Milosevic et al., 2020; Vreja et al., 2016), or simply bad (Kellerman, 2004).

Songs, as suggested in the previous subsection, can be viewed as a way of introducing a different story. While the loudness of their voices was a desperate attempt for each in that room to want their stories and hurts to be heard, and not succeeding, the song shifted their attention to listening to a different story. It offered them an opportunity to become silent – at least for a little while – and, in silence, to allow the lyrics of a song to wash the dust and dirt away from their souls. Indeed, it was not a paralyzing silence. It was instead a thoughtful and reflective silence. This different story – song – offered participants the possibility of distancing themselves from negative patterns that were keeping them apart, and an opportunity for them to hold themselves together differently. The capacity to tell a new story is possible because what Curators hold valuable is an awareness and a belief, as Burns (1978) wrote, that 'people can be lifted *into* their better selves' (p. 462; emphasis original) and that they can be lifted to 'higher levels of motivation and morality' (p. 20). Similarly, as Gardner (1969) wrote, it is a conscious awareness that is grounded in the value that people can be lifted 'above the conflicts that tear a society apart and unite them in pursuits of objectives worthy of their best efforts' (p. 134). Imagine the consequences of denying such a value? However, acting on the belief that people can be lifted into their better selves does not guarantee that any desired result(s) will be produced.

Allow me to share Vivian Silver's story. All information about her is gathered from her blogs and what is found in social media. As she wrote in her blog she was born and raised – in my home city, Winnipeg, and she was a 'kibbutz member almost 45 years, the last 28', as she noted, 'on Kibbutz Boen, bordering on the Gaza strip'. Shortly after she graduated from the Hebrew University in Jerusalem, in the late 1960s she dreamed of 'changing the world'. She was also involved in numerous humanitarian groups. She co-founded Women Wage Peace, which advocates for a unified demand for diplomatic negotiation, with full representation of women, to end the Israeli–Palestinian conflict. This passion moved her to spend

> 3½ years in New York, active in Jewish and Zionist causes, including the launch of the Jewish feminist movement in America. It was a life-changing period. During that time, I understood that in addition to being a kibbutz member, I was destined to be a social change and peace activist. (Silver, 2018, para 3)

In 1998, she became the Executive Director of the Negev Institute for Strategies of Peace and Development in Beer Sheva, 'an NGO promoting human sustainable development, shared society between Jews and Arabs and peace in the

Middle East'. What is particularly significant for this social change and peace activist is what infuriated her the most: 'it especially infuriates me when people claim: 'We have no partner on the other side!' I personally know so many Palestinians who yearn for peace no less than we do . . .' (Silver, 2018, para 5). She went on to say:

> I am driven by the intense desire for security and a life of mutual respect and freedom for both our peoples. The thought of yet another war drives me mad. Like the last three, it will not resolve the conflict. It will only bring more dead and wounded. When rockets fall in our area and the media announces that there were no casualties, I want to shout: 'What are you talking about?? **There are thousands of emotionally wounded among us – children and adults alike!** (Silver, 2018, para 6; emphasis original)

In 2016, she wrote:

> Following the three wars with Gaza in the past eight years and coming on the heels of decades of continued bloodshed, too many Israelis have come to believe that we are destined to live by the sword and that there is no hope. They believe that we have no partner and that the Arabs won't give up the struggle until Israel disappears. Many think that those who believe otherwise are naïve at best or traitors at worst. (Silver, 2018, para 5)

Notice for example, stories that are told based on the socialized preconceptions of the other and of the situation at hand, namely that 'we are destined to live by the sword and that there is no hope', or that 'the Arabs won't give up the struggle until Israel disappears'. In these zero-sum stories of sword and survival, where the existence of one precludes the existence of the other, to imagine a different story and to choose to believe otherwise would simply be 'crazy' at best, or traitors at worst. Hence the loyalty of 'we' that is present in this context is a 'we' of 'us against them'. It is this context and storying of the other that led Lederach (2005) to affirm that the best one can do is to take sides in this dualistic struggle. You are either for us or against us. No other options or stories are available. And here's the rub. For all her sincere efforts for peace, Vivian Silver's last text message to her son was, 'They're inside the house'. Her son noted, 'I continued talking with my mother until I heard on the phone screaming and yelling and gunshots outside her window . . . So we stopped talking so (the gunmen) wouldn't hear' (Semple, 2023, para 10; parenthesis original). Vivian Silver was taken hostage by Hamas agents and 'her remains were found shortly after the attack at Kibbutz Be'en, where she lived, but weren't identified until weeks later' (Greenslade, 2023, para 7).

While Vivian Silver believed that people can be lifted *into* their better selves, and while she was infuriated at those who thought otherwise, her being taken hostage and killed affirms that stories that instil anger, resentment, revenge, and rage continue to prevent the transformation of that belief into everyday life, and, by implication, they continue to reinforce violence. Did the Hamas agents know who she was and what she was trying to achieve? We do not know. What we do know is that the rage of violence affirms that acting on the stories we tell ourselves about ourselves and others, can continue to rip communities apart like a sharp double-edged sword and they can at any moment kill persons like Vivian Silver, even though she walked and lived alongside both the Israelis and the Palestinians believing that they can all be partners for peace. Her story affirms that we can edit our stories either for peace or for enmity. She affirmed that editing can be used to confirm or reject the story we tell ourselves about ourselves and about the other.

4.8 Poetry

Poetry could also be used with a view to the non-negotiable orientation to, and relationship with, each other as a *Thou*. It is critical to understand Buber's (1970) distinction between 'I-It' and 'I-Thou'. For him, the attitude of 'I' towards 'It' is one that treats the other not only as an object ('It') but also one that is separate from the 'I'. The attitude of 'I' towards 'Thou' is one in which I-Thou are not separated by discrete bounds. I-Thou is, instead, a living relationship among persons. For Gadamer (1985), the important thing in any human relationship is 'to experience the Thou truly as a Thou – i.e. not to overlook his claim but to let him really say something to us. To this end, openness is necessary' (p. 324). This way of being with the other is also reflected in the African concept of *Ubuntu*. Ubuntu means 'I am what I am because of you'. In Ubuntu culture, 'I' and 'you' are in a relationship with each other. In Ubuntu all relationships is an encounter. The concept of Ubuntu is centred on the principle that my humanity is inextricably caught up in yours – a concept that Archbishop Desmond Tutu described as 'the essence of being human ... I am me because you are you' (as cited in Cantacuzino, 2015, p. 29). We are not islands by ourselves. We are part of a community. Consequently, as co-participants, the healing of a broken community cannot occur without the participation of all because we are all a part of our hurting and suffering community.

But why turn to what might be seen as an unlikely resource like poetry? The poet Robert Frost, for example, as President J.F. Kennedy (1963) noted in his speech at Amherst College,

> coupled poetry and power, for he (Frost) saw poetry as the means of saving power from itself. When power leads men towards arrogance, poetry, reminds him of his limitations. When power narrows the areas of man's concern, poetry reminds him of the richness and diversity of his existence. When power corrupts, poetry cleanses. (Kennedy, 1963, para 1)

Within the context of the brokenness of trust, James Patrick Kinney's (2012) poem *The Cold Within* is particularly useful. Written within the sociopolitical context of the American Civil Rights Movement – when people of colour were fighting for their basic rights as citizens, and for the right to be treated with human dignity – Kinney's (2012) poem continues to be relevant today. Kinney (2012) speaks to the experiences of 'six men' who not only find themselves 'trapped in happen-stance, in bleak and bitter cold' but also amid a 'dying fire in need of logs'. This is how each chose to dwell in bleak and bitter cold. Confronted with the crisis of a dying fire, each man, as Kinney (2012) tells his story, refused to feed the fire with their sticks of birch for different reasons. The first 'held his back', because he noticed 'one was black'. The second 'could not bring himself to give the fire his stick of birch' because he saw one 'not of his church'. A poor man in this group resentfully withheld his log: 'Why should his log be put to use to warm the idle rich?' The rich man, judges the poor as 'lazy' and 'shiftless'. Hence <u>not</u> contributing his log would mean keeping what 'he had earned' to himself and away 'from the lazy shiftless poor'. The 'black man's face' was filled with the spirit of 'revenge'. All this man saw in his stick of wood was 'a chance to spite the white'. And the last of these men in this 'forlorn group' played the transactional game of 'giving only to those who gave'. And since nobody gave, neither did he. Kinney (2012) completes his poem by defining a tragic consequence of this act of withholding:

> *Their logs held tight in human hands was proof of human sin –*
> *They did not die from the cold* without,
> *They died from the cold within.* (as cited in Hawkins, 2012, para 8)

Sharing this poem with those who choose to dwell in peace has often led to moments of silence and disbelief, as expressed through the shaking of their heads. Kinney's (2012) poem taps into a particular aspect of humanity that is experienced today. The act of withholding our 'logs' continues to reinscribe and polarize persons on the basis of racial and religious prejudices (Augoustinos and Reynolds, 2001; Haidt, 2012; Hoffer, 1951/2002). It continues to put humanity in crisis (our dying fire in need of logs). Holding tightly to one's own prejudices, righteousness, resentment, revenge, spite, and transactional giving, continue to perpetuate and sustain one tragic human reality: we all *die from the cold within*. In this 'un-holy' modern-day tragedy, there will be no winners. We will all lose.

5 Peace Leadership as an Affair of the Hands: On Being a Welcoming Presence

Allow me to return to Burns (1978): 'The leader's fundamental act is to induce people to be aware or conscious of what they feel . . . that they can be moved to purposeful action' (Burns, 1978, p. 44). Burns is interpreted as formulating the *purposeful act* of leadership not from the perspective of an instrumental means to an end action, but rather as *leadership as value rational action*, namely that which is 'determined by a conscious belief in the value for its own sake … independently of its prospects for success' (Weber, 1978, pp. 24–25). I offer the possibility of orienting to purposeful action through the metaphor of the Hands.

We use our hands for a number of different purposeful reasons. We use our hands to reach out, welcome and embrace the other in friendship; we shake hands to convey a promise to abide by our promises; a handshake is perceived as being as good as one's word without a single word uttered; we use our hands to sign agreements that are meant to hold us accountable to such hand-signed agreements; we use our hands to push others away or even physically restrain another; we cross our hands (arms) in a show of disagreement or to warm ourselves; we use our hands (fingers) to wipe the tears from our eyes; we use our hands to wave goodbye; we use our hands to cover our ears to stop listening, cover our mouths to stop gossiping, and cover our eyes, to not see what we do not want to see. In all of these hand expressions, we convey a practical demonstration of what it means to dwell in peace (or not).

In saying that purposeful action is essential, we are once again returned to both Burns and Lipman-Blumen's question: 'Leadership for what end?' For Lipman-Blumen, leadership's purpose is clear: peace. Peace/*shalom*, as offered earlier, is expressed in feeling and being-at-home *as if* one is among friends.

5.1 Five Critical Actions

Within the context of the personal story/incident, five critical actions surfaced as both necessary and desirable in response to the disturbance and being-not-at-home. These included (a) consciously breaking any cycle of violence/chaos by stepping away from such circles of intense, emotion-filled disagreement, (b) paying attention to a different story (a different song/hymn), (c) imagining the possibility of being choreographed by a different story/song or language, namely by 'something other' than what presented itself in any acrimonious conversational space, (d) acting on such an imagined 'something other', and finally (e) as will be offered herein, orienting to others 'as-if' all were equal and at the same time honoured in particular. The lived experience of that incident suggests that intentionally disrupting chaos by creating a moment of 'interlude' or, for the technologically literate, 'clicking on the pause key' is a necessary risk and *a* step in facilitating peace. Along with the uncertainty as to what would actually occur, another risk in acting in this manner includes being charged with being crazy ('Are you crazy?'). From this perspective, crazy making, then, is a charge against anyone who is perceived as taking serious matters too lightly. Within the context of the 'incident' for this Element, it is an accusation that believes that peace leaders as dwellers are actually treating one's reality *as if* it was simply a game.

It is here that we turn to an understanding of sociability as formulated by a sociologist, Simmel. For him, sociability 'is the game in which one 'does as if' all were equal, and at the same time, as if one honoured each of them in particular' (Simmel, 1976, p. 86). A philosopher C.S. Lewis made a similar point.

> Do not waste time bothering whether or not you 'love' your neighbor; act as if you did. As soon as we do this, we find one of the great secrets. When you are behaving as if you loved someone, you will presently come to love him. If you injure someone you dislike, you will find yourself disliking him/her more. If you do him/her a good turn, you will find yourself disliking him less. (Lewis, 1972, p. 116)

But is this *attitude* and 'as if' game not a lie or a deception? If I did indeed treat you as an equal and if I did indeed honour you in particular, then why play what seems to look like a pretend 'as if' game? Does this not sow the seeds for manipulation? Simmel (1976) would answer 'yes', *but only if* such a 'game' was 'guided by non-sociable purposes or is designed to disguise such purposes' (p. 86). For him, the game can become a 'lie only when sociable action and speech are made into mere instruments of the intentions and events of practical reality ...' (p. 86). In Aristotle's (1962) language, when action and speech are not made 'for their friends' good, for their friends' sake ...' (Line 1156b, p. 10). Simmel (1976) further went on to acknowledge that the 'actual entanglement of sociability with the events of real life' can 'make such a deception often very tempting' (p. 86). Simmel appears to be returning us to the question that was raised by Burns (1978), namely leadership for *what* end, and *whose* end?' (p. 457). The entanglement of sociability with the event of violence in the Middle East, for example, can be used by some to further their own intentions. In so doing, 'taking sides' becomes one way of demonstrating an unflinching support for one, not for the sake of peace for all, but rather as a means to preserving one's own interests.

Resisting such a temptation depends upon an intentional decision or a choice to be sincerely guided – without wax – by the principle of acting *as if* all were equal and *as if* all deserve to be honoured in particular. While for Simmel, it is a decision that is grounded in the principles of equality and honour, for Aristotle, it is a decision that is rooted in the principle of friendship. Allow me now to offer one story and a poem, one from a scriptural source, and one secular, that show cases both the five critical actions as noted earlier, *and* acting *as if* all were equal, and at the same time, *as if* one honoured each of them in particular. Both the story and the poem speak to the significance and power of the Hands. The power of the Hands offers peace dwellers an opportunity to consider the question of what it would mean to be a Welcoming Presence amid disturbance.

5.2 Stories of Being a Welcoming Presence

5.2.1 The Prodigal Son/the Merciful Father

A story/parable is told in the Gospel of Luke – The Parable of the Prodigal Son. Not only is this parable viewed by Nicoll as being 'perhaps the crown and flower of all the parables' (as cited in Treybig, 2016, para 17) but it is a story that appears *only* in the Gospel of Luke. Perhaps it is not accidental that Luke, who was a physician, would be *the only one* among the other three Gospel writers, to tell a story of what it means to be a Welcoming Presence, namely creating conditions to welcome others home. How is this parable connected to the significance of the Hands? In reflecting on Rembrandt's painting of the *Prodigal Son*, Nouwen (1994) for example, shared:

> I saw a man in great red cloak tenderly touching the shoulders of a disheveled boy kneeling before him. I could not take my eyes away . . . But most of all, it was the hands – the old man's hands – as they touched the boy's shoulders that reached me in a place where I had never been reached before. (p. 4)

The Parable of the Prodigal Son is significant in light of the problem and question posed in this Element because as Nouwen (1994) sub-titled his book, it is 'A Story of Home-Coming'. Here is a story of a father and his two sons. The younger son said to his father: 'Father, let me have the share of the estate that will come to me.' In tolerance, the father did not oppose the arrogance of his son's request. Instead, he divided his property between them and gave the younger son his share of the estate. 'A few days later', the younger son, as the story is told, gathered everything he had and left home, 'for a distant country where he squandered his money on a life of debauchery' (Luke 15: 13). What is the violence that is inherent in the younger son's arrogant request for his share of the inheritance while his father was still alive? The wealth and property of parents are generally shared with one's children and family after one dies. To ask his father for his inheritance while the father was still alive is tantamount to asking his father to consider himself dead. Would not wishing for another to be dead, and acting on that wish, be simply hurtful?

As the story proceeded, this same son 'came to his senses' while living in poverty and 'starving to death' (Luke, 15:17). He decided to return home and ask for his father's forgiveness and acknowledge that he is 'no longer worthy to be called your son' (Luke 15:23). 'But while he was still a long way off', as Luke told his story, 'his father saw him and was filled with compassion for him; he ran to his son, threw his arms around him and kissed him' (Luke 15:20). Compassion, not anger or resentment was his father's response. Expressing his joy that 'this son of mine … who was lost and is found', the father threw his arms around him, kissed him, and chose to 'have a feast and celebrate' (Luke 15:22). He welcomed his son home with unconditional love. Upon seeing this, the elder son 'became angry' (Luke 15: 28). While his father 'pleaded' with him to join in the celebrations, he replied:

> Look! All these years I've been slaving for you and never disobeyed your orders. Yet you never gave me even a young goat so I could celebrate with my friends. But when this son of yours who has squandered your property with prostitutes comes home, you kill the fattened calf for him! (Luke 29–30)

The elder son, who did not leave home, who did not treat his father as if he was dead, and who 'never disobeyed' his father's orders, was not recognized for his loyalty and obedience. He lived his life by dotting every 'i' and crossing every 't' of loyalty and duty, and yet there was no young goat or celebration for his staying home, staying loyal and dutiful. We can understand his anger and resentment. We might even say that it was natural for him to be angry, bitter, and resentful, and that he was justified for not wanting to have anything to do with the celebrations and for refusing to go into to his father's house – 'he refused to go in' (Luke 15: 28). In his resentment, he did not refer to his brother as being his brother but rather as 'this son of yours'. In so doing, he constructed a distance or a 'wall' between him, his father, and his brother. In a curious way, we are returned to the question of 'who is right and who is wrong?' that was raised in von Foerster's story. The elder son was convinced that he was right because he did all that was deemed to be right. He obeyed the rules to a 't'. And by implication, 'this son of yours' is wrong because he did all that was deemed to be wrong. He disobeyed the rules. He cheated his own father for wanting, receiving, and squandering his share of his father's inheritance.

In throwing his arms (Hands) around his errant younger son's homecoming, the father shifts our attention away from this dualistic either-or world right or wrong. This purposeful act of wrapping his arms around his son with compassion, kissing him and joyfully welcoming him home, led Pope Francis (2016) to reframe the parable of the Prodigal Son to the parable of the Merciful Father. The Merciful Father forgives. What is also noteworthy is that Pope Francis went one step further in saying that 'when one feels righteous', as in 'I always did the right thing', this 'attitude of feeling 'right' is the wrong attitude: it is pride'

(Pope Francis, 2016, para 3). Dutifully following the rules and expecting to be rewarded by such a following is also characteristic of a transactional relation to following the rules. Following the rules, in other words, is viewed by the elder son, as a means to an end. It is instrumental and transactional in that he acted in his calculated interest of getting what he expected to receive. He expected to receive goats, fattened calves, and celebrations. Not getting what he expected resulted in anger and resentment.

In being a welcoming presence, the merciful father in this parable was choreographed by different values which included compassion, mercy, and forgiveness. The merciful father welcomed both his sons. He did not discount or become angry at his elder son: 'My son, you are always with me, and everything I have is yours' (Luke 15:31). While Burns (1978) believed that we 'can be lifted to our better selves' (p. 462), the merciful father demonstrates what this 'better self' could look like in the context of the violence of wishing him dead by his younger son, and in the context of the resentment of his elder son. What cannot be discounted, however, is that anger, resentment, pride, arrogance, tolerance, mercy, compassion, and forgiveness, all reside or dwells in one's heart. Which value(s) we choose to choreograph our lives, our leadership, our relationship to all around us, and to our past is ours to make. In the story of the parable of the Prodigal Son/Merciful Father, the father did not deliberate and choose from the perspective of the past but rather from the imagination of the now, the future, and what could be possible. In Aristotle's (1962) terms:

> No object of choice belongs to the past . . . For deliberation does not refer to the past but only to the future and to what is possible; and it is not possible that what is past should not have happened. Therefore, Agathon is right when he says: 'One thing alone is denied even to god, to make undone the deeds which have been done.' (Aristotle, 1962, Line 1139b, pp. 10–14)

The consequences of past actions, by virtue of being past, cannot be undone. For Agathon, changing the past – this thing alone – even god cannot undo. We only live in the present, and how we choose to dwell purposefully in the present amid our inability to undo the consequences of past actions, will influence how we will *be* with each other in the future. At the same time, it cannot be denied that we can also choose – in our here and now – to deliberate on how we relate to our past especially when the consequences of hurtful and painful events of the past cannot be undone. Within the context of the parable, the merciful father chose to welcome his younger son home while continuing to acknowledge that all that he possessed also belonged to the elder son. He did not relate to his past with hurt or anger, and least of all, with regret. He did not hold his younger son back from his decision to leave home. Although he may have known the pain that would come to his son, his love for his son prevented him from doing so. To have done so would in effect mean forcing his son to stay at home. That was a choice that belonged to his younger son and his father respected that. Nouwen (1994) wrote that as father,

> The only authority he claims for himself is the authority of compassion. That authority comes from letting the sins of his children pierce his heart … From the deep inner place where love embraces (his sons) … the father reaches out to his children. The touch of his hands radiating inner light, seeks only to heal. (p. 95)

Nouwen (1994) interprets the touch of father's hands in embracing his son who has come home as being 'the instruments of the father's inner eye' (p. 94), radiating, as he said, an inner light for the sake of healing. Said differently, in being a welcoming presence, he enables conditions for healing. It is a seeing that deeply understands the restlessness of his sons (and humanity?), a seeing that knows with immense compassion the suffering of those who have chosen to leave home in the manner in which his younger son did, a seeing that enables the father to celebrate with joy his son's coming home, and a seeing that allowed him to also affirm the elder son's decision to stay at home. In this way, this purposeful act is connected to the affair of the heart.

5.2.2 The Touch of a Master's Hand

The significance of the Hands is also extrapolated by Mary Brooks Welch through her poem *The Touch of a Master's Hand*. A grey-haired man, an auctioneer, the crowd in an auction, and an inanimate object 'a battered and scarred violin' are the main characters in her poem. Even though the auctioneer was convinced that auctioning this sorry-looking violin was 'scarcely worth his while', he went through the motions. After all, that was what he was paid to do. The highest bidder offered $3.00 confirming that the violin was not worth much at all. As Welch's poem proceeded, a second before the auctioneer declared 'sold' ('Going for three …') a grey-haired man came forward and interrupted the auctioneering process. This grey-haired man 'picked up the bow, dusted the old violin, tightened its loose strings', and 'played a melody so pure and sweet, As sweet as the caroling angels sing'. When 'the music ceased', the auctioneer touched by what he saw and heard, restarted the auction with a 'voice quiet and low'. He was surprised to receive a highest bid of $3,000. Sold! 'What changed its worth?' the crowd cried. 'Swift came the reply: "The touch of a master's hand".' At this point in her poem, Welch poetically shifts our attention to not only seeing a 'battered and scarred violin' as being akin to seeing 'many a man whose life is out of tune', but also that such humans are also 'auctioned cheap to a thoughtless crowd'. The significance of the power of the Hand is captured in her closing stanza:

> But the Master comes, and the foolish crowd
> Never can quite understand
> The worth of a soul and the change that is wrought
> By the touch of the Master's hand.

Like the Parable of the Prodigal Son or the Merciful Father, Welch also reminds us of the power of the Hands as the Hands are guided by the inner eye of the Heart. While the folly of a 'foolish crowd' makes a judgement on the basis of appearances, while they judged a book by its cover, the wisdom of the heart's inner eye understands the worth of a human's soul and the possibility of change that can be 'wrought' by the touch of a master's hands. The purposeful actions identified throughout this Element are rooted in Welch's understanding of the worth of a human soul.

In both Luke's Parable and Welch's Poem, we notice a consistent theme. Purposeful Action (**H**ands) is displayed by (a) consciously breaking any cycle of violence/chaos by stepping away from such circles of intense, emotion-filled disagreement, (b) paying attention to a different story (a different song/hymn), (c) imagining the possibility of being choreographed by that different a song/story or language, namely by something other than what presented itself in any acrimonious conversational space, (d) acting on such an imagination and (e) orienting to others 'as-if' all were equal and at the same time honoured in particular. Both the Merciful Father and the Grey-Haired Man (Master) acted *as if* the sons and human beings who are battered and scarred and out of tune, like the old violin, are worthy of honour and respect. Within the context of St. Francis' Prayer of Peace, the Merciful Father and the Grey-Haired Man were able to be a channel of God's peace, because they 'madly' ('Are you crazy?') believed that human beings who appear in their worlds with violence can be lifted into their better selves.

Burns (1978) also joins in the chorus of these 'as-ifs' when he concluded his volume on *Leadership*, with his 'practical advice'. We need to live with each other, he advised, by 'treat(ing) ... all persons like *persons*' (Burns, 1978, p. 462; emphasis original) and not *like* pawns or things to be manipulated, enslaved, controlled, discarded, or killed. Treating persons *like* persons is his way of saying treat persons *as if* they are persons, namely as a 'Thou', and not as an 'It' (Buber, 1970), worthy of honour and respect. This is a principled, sacred, and non-negotiable gift that persons give to each other and owe one another. And in so dwelling, dwellers demonstrate their care for the well-being of all and how they choose to spare and safeguard each other from harm and danger.

6 Peace Leadership as an Affair of the Holy: On Being a Neighbour

These actions based on the 'as if' invitation *to dwell in peace* brings us into the realm of the Spiritual/ Holy or what we hold as sacred. This is an integral feature of the dwelling place of peace dwellers. This is their home. And, as gracious hosts, they invite all to not only to make themselves to feel at home in this dwelling place but also to live in community. It is in this way, as Kornfield (1993) noted, they acknowledge that 'true community arises when we can speak in accord with truth and compassion. This sense spiritual community is a wondrous part of what heals and transforms us on our path' (p. 24). True and spiritual community then is what peace/*shalom*, as true friendship, hopes to achieve. It requires that we treat persons as persons *as if* all were equal, and at the same time, *as if* one honoured each of them in particular' (Simmel, 1976, p. 86). Arendt (2005), however, reminds us that acting *as if* all are equal 'does not mean that friends become the same or equal to each other, but rather that they become equal partners in a common world – that they together constitute a community' (p. 17). In this way, as equal partners, no one seeks to prevail over the other because they all share in their attempts to live as equal partners in a common world.

All of the three Hs (Head, Hearts, Hands) that we worked with in this Element preserved what is Holy in one way or another. Whether it was a matter of dwelling in peace from the perspective of what it means to be a Guardian (Head) or dwelling in peace by inducing others to feel the need to care and be Curators (Heart), or to dwell in peace by opening one's arms to not judge the other but for creating conditions where others can feel welcomed (Hands), all were guided by and rooted in the sacred spirit and principles of shalom, friendship, care, and healing. From the perspective of the fourth H, **H**oly, peace dwellers understand and accept the summon to embrace the affairs of the Head, Heart, and Hands, when confronted with pain and hurt no matter where they are and, as will be described next, it adds its own soulful principle. In this way they become 'partners' (Burns, 2003) in their transformative efforts towards peace – partnering with a transforming purpose. From the perspective of the Holy, what would such partnering and transforming purpose look like in everyday life?

6.1 The Art of Being a Neighbour

In response to this question, allow me to turn to yet another story that, again, appears *only* in Luke's Gospel. Commonly called The Good Samaritan, the soulful and healing presence of human beings to other human beings, offers us a practical example of the holiness of treating each other *like* persons, *like* friends, or in Luke's story *like* a neighbour. In response to a 'test' question by a legal expert: 'Who is My Neighbour?' Jesus told this story.

> A man was going down from Jerusalem to Jericho when he was attacked by robbers. They stripped him of his clothes, beat him and went away, leaving him half dead. A priest happened to be going down the same road, and when he saw the man, he passed by on the other side. So too, a Levite, when he came to the place and saw him, passed by on the other side. But a Samaritan, as he traveled, came where the man was; and when he saw him, he took pity on him. He went to him and bandaged his wounds, pouring on oil and wine. Then he put the man on his own donkey, brought him to an inn and took care of him. The next day he took out two denarii and gave them to the innkeeper. 'Look after him,' he said, 'and when I return, I will reimburse you for any extra expense you may have'.
>
> Which of these three do you this was a neighbour to the man who fell into the hands of the robbers?
>
> The expert in the law replied, 'The one who had mercy on him.
>
> Jesus told him, 'Go and do likewise.' (Luke, 10:30–35)

In this story, Jesus makes a political decision in distinguishing the actions of the priest, Levite, and the Samaritan. At his time (and now?), Samaritans were seen as being enemies to the Jews. Recall for example, the story of a woman from Samaria who came to draw water from a well. As John narrated that story:

> When a Samaritan woman came to draw water, Jesus said to her, 'Will you give me a drink?' (His disciples had gone into the town to buy food). The Samaritan woman said to him, 'You are a Jew, and I am a Samaritan woman. How can you ask me for a drink?' (For Jews do not associate with Samaritans) ... Just then his disciples returned and were surprised to find him talking with a woman. But no one asked, 'What do you want?' or 'Why are you talking with her?' (John, 4:7–27)

The Jews (Judeans) of his time were most concerned about the purity of their bloodlines, namely, that everyone in that community could trace their history to Jacob, son of Isaac, and grandson of Abraham. They believed that they would become 'unclean' if they associated with Samaritans who readily intermarried. They thought that they would become unclean in the eyes of their God if they travelled on Samaritan roads or drank from Samaritan wells. In this context, we can understand how livid they might have been in hearing or seeing Jesus, another Jew and Judean, associating with a Samaritan woman and asking her for a drink. Jesus' disciples were themselves 'surprised' to find him talking with a woman from Samaria. But although they were 'surprised', they chose not to pursue it any further.

We can better understand Luke and Jesus' political decision in telling the story of the Good Samaritan within the context of the Judaeans' relationship with Samaritans. The Levite and the priest, who happened to travel down the same road where a wounded man lay, absorbed by their institutional roles, went about their religious business of not contaminating themselves by not making the wounded man their business. They chose instead to walk pass by him 'on the other side'. In so doing, they showed that they were preoccupied to the point that they made themselves unavailable for the surprise of an encounter. Was this the story that Brecht (1937) had in mind as he wrote in his poem 'To Posterity?' He asked the question: 'And he who walks calmly across the street, Is he not out of reach of his friends, In trouble?' (Stanza 2). Unencumbered by any role, institutional, religious, or otherwise, the Samaritan, when he came to that same place and saw that wounded man, 'took pity on him . . . went to him and bandaged his wounds, pouring on oil and wine (and) brought him to an inn and took care of him'. This was his direct person-to-person encounter.

Who then is my neighbour? In this story, Luke affirms that neighbours are not those who live beside one's home, let alone those who live on one's street. Whereas social science researchers have focused on the science and sociology of neighbourhoods, the art of Being a Neighbour, as Ricouer (1965) disclosed, situates us 'between a sociology of human relationships and a theology of charity' (p. 98). He further went on to say: 'If there is no sociology of the neighbour, perhaps there is a sociology which starts out from the frontier of the neighbour' (p. 98).

In Luke's story/parable, a critical learning that emerges from the 'frontier of the neighbor' is that one does not *have* neighbours. Neighbours are not 'things' to be possessed. Neighbours are not social objects. To orient to the social fact of neighbour as a 'thing' would in effect move us to a study of neighbourhoods and/or a study of 'types' of neighbours. Instead, as Luke affirms through this story/parable, being a neighbour 'lies in the habit of making oneself available' (Ricouer, 1965, p. 95) to others where they are, including being present to the wounded, to the dispossessed, and to those who are hurting. The significance of Ricoeur's use of the word 'habit' cannot be underestimated. While there may be good or bad habits, what they both share in common is a constant practice that becomes a 'usual' way of being. If this is so, then Ricouer shares in Hegel's (2007) understanding of 'subjective spirit'. 'Habit,' Hegel (2007) said, 'is the most essential feature of the existence of all mental life,' because it enables 'religious content, moral content, etc., to belong to this self, as this soul, in its very being' (p. 202). Within this context then, the habit of being a neighbour as the spirit of making oneself available is harmonized (becomes one) in the subject through the *practiced conduct* of making oneself available. Habits are not a consequence of a singular act. Habits are formed by repeated actions. By virtue of this, the habit of making oneself available could becomes 'usual' to the point that one may no longer be aware that *making oneself available* is the very principle that guides Neighbours to be neighbours. It is a conduct that comes to them 'naturally' *as if* they are in tune with nature's way of being.

Like the Samaritan, peace dwellers also make themselves available by being present to the other – person to person. They make themselves available by being open to changing one's own itinerary in the face of unexpected events, like, stumbling upon a person who was beaten and left half-dead, or in confronting voices of anger, dissent, and hurt, as that is told in the personal story for this Element. As neighbours they make themselves available by *dwelling in-between* the sociology of human relationships and a theology of charity. From the perspective of the sociology of human relationships, they make themselves available in their spontaneity when confronted with unforeseen and conflicted events. They invent and reinvent themselves within the context that surrounds them, and they open themselves to being surprised by what may transpire. In this way, peace leaders as Neighbours compose an improvised response and a life.

For Mary Catherine Bateson (1989), the art of improvisation, rather than technical design, offers Neighbours the flexibility of 'recombining partly familiar materials' in ways that are 'sensitive to *context, interaction, and response*' (p. 2; emphasis added). In such improvisations they appeal to what is and is not familiar. While improvisation may be familiar to many, the theology of charity may sound strange. From the perspective of a theology of charity, Neighbours ground their practice of making themselves available in the sacred principle (value) of *agape*. In Christianity, *agape* is 'the highest form of love, charity' and 'the love of God for man and man for God' (Liddell and Scott, 1901, p. 6)

What must be highlighted in the Parable of the Good Samaritan is that, for Jesus, it is not only a story about the goodwill of the Samaritan, but also a call for action ('Go and do likewise') – a call to act with an empowering and transforming purpose. This story, in other words, calls us to reflect on the questions: (i) *what does this mean* to make ourselves available where polarization and divisions constantly increases, and where it seems that we do not live in the world of the 'neighbour?' and (ii) what can we do about it? It is a call to conduct ourselves in the direct relationship of 'person to person' within the context of where we find ourselves in relation to each other, and not simply through the mediation of institutions, including the mediations of a legal system.

By implication, the direct relationship of *person to person* within the social context of wherever we find ourselves, and our particular situations, returns us to a micro and local level. It is in the frontier of these localized instances that we begin to engage in the practice and habit of dwelling in peace – one relationship at a time, one encounter at a time, one act of charity at a time. It does not however stop there. Beginning with our direct relationship with one another, this also means that we extend such a relationship with our own family members, with legal systems as they are established by the states and nations, with organizational/political structures that divide more than unify, with others who may look different from me, with others who may be members of different religions, and so forth. Indeed, the habit of being a neighbour cannot not include all who have vested interests in any concord or discord – socially, politically, and economically.

The lived experience of being neighbour, as it is told in Luke's parable can be received as appealing to the awakening of our own consciousness to the power of charity. If being a neighbour through acts of charity is lacking at a micro and local person to person level, such a lack will naturally extend to larger macro levels of any society. It is precisely in cases where there is an absence of charity – potentially or in reality – that we need an institution of laws and rules to protect persons against the uncharitable acts of other persons. Laws aim at deterring persons from harming other persons. Without disavowing the need laws, we cannot dismiss the idea that the presence of laws and legal institutions protects all (at least in intention) from the absence of charity. Similarly, the presence of violence in our societies also affirms the absence of charity. Choosing to pass by each other on the other side of the road with an attitude of indifference affirms the absence of charity. Alternatively, a simple nod of the head upon passing someone on a street can affirm the presence of another person. Not a single nod, but repeated nods that allow a nod to become a habit. A person's genuine and repeated nods are a step that can potentially begin a longer journey of neighbourliness.

7 Concluding Thoughts

The context of the lived experiences of persons in a particular 'incident' was offered as a microcosm of the challenge confronting peace dwellers. Emerging from this 'case' or 'incident' were the questions and problem of peace leadership, namely, how we choose to dwell decisively and imaginatively in the in-between space of being-at-home and being-not-at-home (restlessness), and how we choose to be governed by the interrelated purposes of the Head, Heart, Hands, and Holy. Insofar as restlessness is a human condition, then, an argument is made that it is not a matter of eliminating restlessness but rather the work we do to restore a sense of equilibrium in the context of our human experience of being-at-home and being-not-at-home.

In offering the fourfold peace leadership framework to aid in this process of restoration, some liberty was taken to reconstruct Burns' (1978) formulation of the essential and fundamental act of a leader, with the understanding that leadership is a relationship between and among leaders and followers. Within our leadership literature, to the best of my knowledge, Burns' understanding of the fundamental act of leadership has not been interpreted from the perspective of the interrelationship and interconnectedness of the affairs of the Head, Heart, Hands, and Holy. My hope is that the reconstructed formulation of leadership, as offered in this Element, will open another way of thinking about the theory and practice of peace leadership.

The questions and problem of peace dwelling are rooted in the notion that we are all *dwellers*. What emerged from this 'case study' or 'incident' is that in times of peace and disturbance, peace dwellers, leaders, and followers are called to surrender themselves *to being governed* by four ways of being: (i) Being a Guardian by caring, preserving, and safeguarding each other from harm and danger; (ii) Being a Curator by creating conditions for healing; (iii) Being a Welcoming Presence, by responding to disturbance with compassion; and (iv) Being a Neighbour by make it a habit (practiced conduct) to make oneself available to others in times of harmony and disharmony. Figure 2 reconstructs the fourfold connectedness of peace leadership and peace dwelling within the unique character of these four ways of being.

This is peace dwellers sacred in-between dwelling place. They dwell in-between the spaces of the head (being a guardian), heart (being a curator), hand (being a welcoming presence), and holy (being a neighbour). They each relate to each other and take each other into account in this in-between space rather than

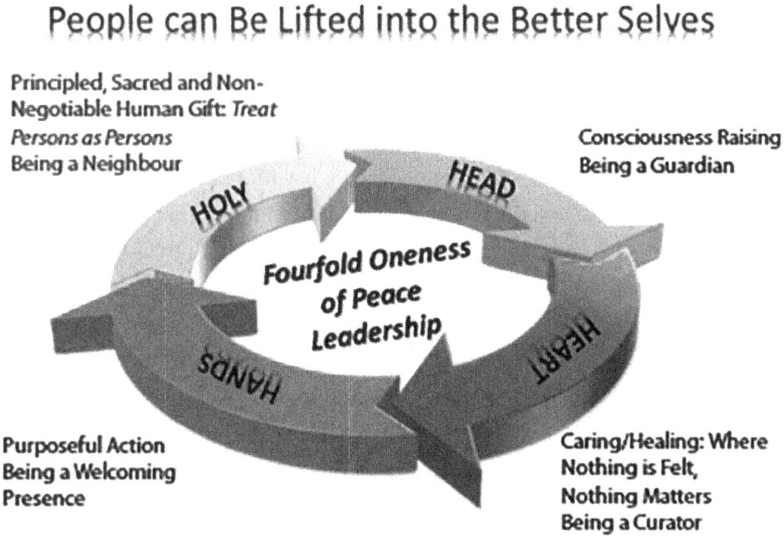

Figure 2 Relationship between four Hs and four ways of being

exist independently of each other. Peace leadership, then, is not about governing or ruling others, and neither is it about solving the problem of disturbance. Returning to Burns (1978) we also saw that the decision to surrender ourselves to being governed by these four ways of being or practices is rooted in another value. Recall, for example, that the language of practical/practices is not understood in terms of 'how-to' but rather as a 'choice and decision between possibilities' and as 'always [having] a relationship to a person's being' (Gadamer, 1996c, pp. 3–4).

What peace dwellers hold valuable is a belief that 'people can be lifted *into* their better selves' (Burns, 1978, p. 462; emphasis original), and, as Gardner (1969) wrote, that they can 'lifted above the conflicts that tear a society apart and unite them in pursuits of objectives worthy of their best efforts' (p. 134), and that peoples' hearts can be radically transformed from hearts of stone to hearts of flesh (Ezekiel, 36:26). This is a radical choice and decision that peace dwellers make amid many other possibilities. It is a radical choice that defines their way to being in the world. Indeed, if the fundamental act of leadership is raising the consciousness of both leaders and followers by meaningfully defining their values because 'values exist only where there is consciousness' (Langer, as cited in Burns, 1978, p. 44), then to choose this value or belief (starting point) is to choose to be governed by the interrelationship between and among being a guardian, curator, welcoming presence and neighbour. In saying this, I do not mean to construct a theory of causation, in the conventional scientific and lineal sense of cause and effect, where a series of arguments and effects do not come back to the starting point. Instead, as offered by Bateson (1979), the four ways of being are viewed as standing in a recursive and reciprocal relationship with each other and with this underlying belief/value – where effects come back to the starting-point and *vice versa*. Figure 3 visualizes this recursive relation in the form of an infinity diagram.

As narrated in the story of Vivian Silver, what must be stressed is that we cannot force people to believe that they and others can be lifted *into* their better selves, and neither can we force them to lift themselves into their better selves. Therein lies the limit of such a value/belief. Dwelling in peace is always risky and messy. Because of the presence of violence over the centuries, it appears as if human beings are more willing to hang on to past hurts and pain; it appears as if human beings demonstrate a greater propensity to take what is not theirs in a zero-sum game of survival; it appears as if vengeance and revenge are dominant aspects in our human lives. In this context, as Vivian Silver (2018) painfully acknowledged: 'most residents in our areas', residents who have been and are in a constant struggle for peace, 'have sunk into despair, become cynical or tried to bury their heads in the sand' (para 3). It is in times like this that peace

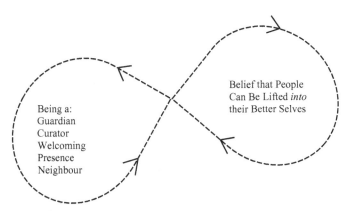

Figure 3 Recursive relationship between underlying value/belief
and ways of being

dwellers are summoned to take personal and collective responsibility to be a guardian, to be a curator of hearts and souls, to be a welcoming presence, and to be a neighbour. Imagine peace leadership in the absence of any of these four ways of being.

Finally, we can learn much from the boy in von Forester's story who did ordinary things with his neighbours. What was 'extraordinary' in his ordinary way of living was that his practices were 'foreign' among those who lived on different sides of the street. To this end, in our own Here and Now, in our own local places, in paying heed to the Peace Prayer of St. Francis, to the ordinary actions of the boy, and in accepting a human adage that we reap what we sow: Where there is hatred, what would it mean for us to sow love? Where there is despair, what would it mean for us to sow hope? Where there is darkness, what would it mean for us to sow light? Where there is sadness, what would it mean for us to sow joy?

I sincerely hope that the four practices of being a guardian, curator, welcoming presence, and neighbour, offered in this Element will be embraced and embodied in mind (head) heart, body (hands) and soul (holy), for the sake of dwelling in peace. Imagine the possibilities for peace, if we each gave ourselves the gift to pause, to stay silent, reflect, and learn to sincerely embrace all four practices of dwelling in peace. If this call for a shared imagination and action amid violence and disturbance sounds 'crazy' (not real – 'are you crazy?'), so be it. For the sake of peace and for the sake of dwelling in peace, perhaps we need to risk 'crazy-making' in a really mad and messy world. If not us, then who? If not now, then when?

Peace Be With You. Make Yourselves At Home.

References

Al-Mughrabi, N. (2023). Gaza death toll tops 10,000; UN calls it a children's graveyard. www.reuters.com/world/middle-east/pressure-israel-over-civil ians-steps-up-ceasefire-calls-rebuffed-2023-11-06/

Amaladas, S. (2018). *Intentional leadership: Getting to the heart of the matter.* Taylor & Francis.

Amaladas, S. (2019). *Leadership studies: A desire for shared agreement.* Cambridge Elements, Cambridge University Press.

Arendt, H. (1958). *The human condition.* The University of Chicago Press.

Arendt, H. (2005). *The promise of politics.* Schocken Books.

Arendt, H. (2018). Action and the 'Pursuit of Happiness'. In J. Kohn (Ed.), *Thinking without a banister* (pp. 201–219). Schocken Books.

Aristotle. (1962). *Nichomachean ethics.* (M. Oswald, Trans.). The Bobbs-Merrill.

Augoustinos, M., & Reynolds, K. J. (2001). *Understanding prejudice, racism, and social conflict.* Sage.

Barbour, J. D. (2006). Burns, J. M. *Encyclopedia of educational leadership and administration* (pp. 93–94). Sage.

Bartimote, H. (2020). Leaders: How well do you balance your head and heart? https://blog.container-solutions.com/leaders-how-well-do-you-balance-your-head-and-heart

Bateson, G. (1979). *Mind and nature: A necessary unity.* E. P. Dutton.

Bateson, G. (2000). *Steps to ecology of mind.* The University of Chicago Press.

Bateson, G., & Bateson, M. C. (1987). *Angels fear.* Macmillan.

Bateson, M. C. (1989). *Composing a life.* Grove Press.

Becvar, R., & Becvar, D. (2018). Facilitating peace: Perspectives from ecosystemic family therapy. In S. Amaladas & S. Byrne (Eds.), *Peace leadership: A quest for connectedness* (pp. 15–29). Routledge.

Brecht, B. (1937). To posterity. https://allpoetry.com/To-Posterity

Brox, J. (2019). *Silence.* Houghton Mifflin Harcourt.

Buber, M. (1970). *I and Thou.* (W. Kaufmann, Trans.). Charles Scribner.

Burns, J. M. (1978). *Leadership.* Harper & Row.

Burns, J. M. (2003). *Transforming leadership.* Grove Press.

Burns, J. M. (2006). Afterword. In G. R. Goethals & G. J. Sorenson (Eds.), *A quest for a general theory of leadership* (pp. 234–239). Edward Elgar.

Campbell, J. (1949). *The hero with a thousand faces.* MJF Books.

Cantacuzino, M. (2015). *The forgiveness project: Stories for a vengeful age.* Jessica Kingsley.

Carlyle, T. (1841/1993). *On heroes, hero-worship, & the heroic in history*. University of California Press.

Durkheim, E. (1966). *The rules of sociological method*. (S. Lukes, Ed.). The Free Press.

Estes, R. (2017). The search for well-being: From ancient to modern times. In R. Estes & J. Sirgy (Eds.), *The pursuit of human well-being: The untold global history* (pp. 3–30). Springer International.

Flemons, D. (1991). *Completing distinctions*. Shambala.

Freire, P. (1970). *Pedagogy of the oppressed*. Seabury Press.

Frost, R. (1914). *Mending Wall*. www.poetryfoundation.org/poems/44266/mending-wall

Gadamer, H.-G. (1985). *Truth and method*. Crossroads.

Gadamer, H.-G. (1996). *The enigma of health: The art of healing in a scientific age*. (J. Gaiger & N. Walker, Trans.). Stanford University Press.

Gadamer, H.-G. (1996a). Anxiety and Anxieties. In H.-G. Gadamer (Ed.), *The enigma of health: The art of healing in a scientific age*. (J. Gaiger & N. Walker, Trans.) (pp. 152–162). Stanford University Press.

Gadamer, H.-G. (1996b). Bodily experience and the limits of objectification. In H.-G. Gadamer, *The enigma of health: The art of healing in a scientific age*. (J. Gaiger & N. Walker, Trans.) (pp. 70–82). Stanford University Press.

Gadamer, H.-G. (1996c). Theory, technology, praxis. In H.-G. Gadamer, *The enigma of health: The art of healing in a scientific age*. (J. Gaiger & N. Walker, Trans.) (pp. 1–30). Stanford University Press.

Gadamer, H.-G. (1996d). The problem of intelligence. In H.-G. Gadamer, *The enigma of health: The art of healing in a scientific age*. (J. Gaiger & N. Walker, Trans.) (pp. 45–60). Stanford University Press.

Gadamer, H.-G. (1996e). Apologia for the art of healing. In H.-G. Gadamer, *The enigma of health: The art of healing in a scientific age*. (J. Gaiger & N. Walker, Trans.) (pp. 31–44). Stanford University Press.

Gadamer, H.-G. (1996f). Treatment and Dialogue. In H.-G. Gadamer (Ed.), *The enigma of health: The art of healing in a scientific age*. (J. Gaiger & N. Walker, Trans.) (pp. 125–140). Stanford University Press.

Galtung, J. (1964). An editorial. *Journal of Peace Research*, *1*(1), 1–4.

Galtung, J. (2001). After violence, reconstruction, reconciliation, and resolution: Coping with visible and invisible effects of war and violence. In M. Abu-Nimer (Ed.), *Reconciliation, justice, and coexistence: Theory & practice* (pp. 3–23). Lexington Books.

Gardner, J. W. (1969). *No easy victories*. Harper & Row.

Gibran, K. (1923/2020). On marriage. In K. Gibran (Ed.), *The prophet*. Alfred A. Knopf.

Gillespie, A., & Patman, R. G. (2023). As the Israel-Gaza crisis worsens, what are NZ's diplomatic options. www.rnz.co.nz/news/world/501156/as-the-israel-gaza-crisis-worsens-what-are-nz-s-diplomatic-options

Givey, D. (2009). *The social thought of Thomas Merton*. St. Mary's Press.

Glaser, C. (1990). *Analyzing strategic nuclear policy*. Princeton University Press.

Graen, G., & Uhl-Bien, M. (1995). Relationship-based approach to leadership: Development of leader-member exchange (LMX) theory of leadership over 25 years: Applying a multi-level multi-domain perspective. *The Leadership Quarterly, 6*(2), 219–247. https://doi.org/10.1016/1048-9843(95)90036-5

Greenslade, B. (2023). Vivian Silver, activist killed in Hamas attack, remembered as peacemaker at Winnipeg memorial. www.cbc.ca/news/canada/manitoba/vivian-silver-winnipeg-activist-killed-hamas-1.7059642

Grint, K. (2005). *Leadership: Limits and possibilities*. Palgrave Macmillan.

Grint, K. (Ed.) (2007). *Leadership: Classical, contemporary, and critical Approaches*. Oxford University Press.

Guthey, E., Kempster, S., & Remke, R. (2018). Leadership for what? In R. Riggio (Ed.), *What's wrong with leadership?* (pp. 279–281). Taylor & Francis.

Habermas, J. (1984). *The theory of communicative action*. Vol. 2. The Beacon Press.

Haidt, J. (2012). *The righteous mind: Why good people are divided by politics and religion*. Random House.

Hawkins, S. (2012). The Cold within by James Patrick Kinney: Poem, Purpose, Progress. www.allthingsif.org/archives/1405

Hegel, G. W. F. (2007). *Lectures on the philosophy of spirit 1827–8*. (R. R. Williams, Trans.). Oxford University Press.

Heidegger, M. (1995). *The fundamental concepts of metaphysics: World, finitude, solitude*. (W. McNeill & N. Walker, Trans.). Indiana University Press.

Heidegger, M. (1977). Building, dwelling, thinking. In D. Krell (Ed.), *Basic writings* (pp. 323–339). Harper & Row.

Heifetz, R., & Linsky, M. (2017). Sacred heart. In R. Heifetz & M. Linsky (Eds.), *Leadership on the line* (pp. 226–236). Harvard Business Review Press.

Hobbes, T. (1642/2017). *De Cive*. Anodos Books.

Hobbes, T. (1651/1977). *Leviathan*. Penguin Classics.

Hoffer, E. (1951/2002). *The true believer: Thoughts on the nature of mass movements*. Harper Collins.

Human Rights Watch. (2013). *World report 2013: Israel/Palestine*. www.hrw.org/world-report/2013/country-chapters/israel/palestine

Kant, I. (1785/1956). *Groundwork of the metaphysic of morals*. (H. J. Paton, Trans.). Harper & Row.

Katz, R. L. (1955). Skills of an effective administrator. *Harvard Business Review, 33*(1), 33–42.

Kellerman, B. (2004). *Bad leadership*. Harvard Business Review Press.

Kennedy, J. F. (1963). President John F. Kennedy: Remarks at Amherst College, 26 October. www.arts.gov/about/kennedy-transcript

Kinney, J. P. (2012). The cold within. In S. Hawkins (Ed.), The cold within by James Patrick Kinney: Poem, purpose, progress. www.allthingsif.org/arch ives/1405

Kirkpatrick, S. A., & Locke, E. A. (1991). Leadership: Do traits matter? *The Executive, 5*, 48–60.

Kornfield, J. (1993). *A path with heart: A guide through the perils and promises of spiritual life*. Bantam Books.

Kouzes, J., & Posner, B. (2017). *The leadership challenge*. (6th Ed.). Wiley.

Kuhnert, K., & Lewis, P. (1987). Transactional and transformational leadership: A constructive/developmental analysis. *Academy of Management Review, 12*(4), 648–657.

Kuhnert, K. W. (1994). Transforming leadership: Developing people through delegation. In B. M. Bass & B. J. Avolio (Eds.), *Improving organizational effectiveness through transformational leadership* (pp. 10–25). Sage.

Ladner, K. (2009). Take 35: Reconciling constitutional orders. In A. M Timpson (Ed.), *First nations, first thoughts: The impact of Indigenous thought in Canada* (pp. 279–300). UBC Press.

Lederach, J. P. (2005). *The moral imagination: The art and soul of building peace*. Oxford University Press.

Lederach, J. P. (2017). *Building peace: Sustainable reconciliation in divided societies*. United States Institute of Peace.

Leonardsson, H., & Rudd, G. (2015). The 'local' turn in peacebuilding: A literature review of effective and emancipatory local peacebuilding. *Third World Quarterly, 36*(5), 825–839.

Lewis, C. S. (1972). *Mere Christianity*. Harper Collins.

Liddell, H. G., & Scott, R. (1901). ἀγάπη. *A Greek-English Lexicon*. Clarendon Press.

Lindsay, J., & Gartzke, E. (2019). *Introduction: Cross-domain deterrence, from practice to theory*. Oxford University Press. https://doi.org/10.1093/oso/ 9780190908645.003.0001. ISBN *978-0-19-090960-4*

Lipman-Blumen, J. (2006). *The allure of toxic leaders*. Oxford University Press.

Lopez, B. (2020). *Horizon*. Vintage Canada.

Love, C. (2005). Using both head and heart for effective leadership. *Journal of Family & Consumer Sciences, 9*(2), 17–19.

Lumsden, M. (1999). Breaking the cycle of violence. *Journal of Peace Research*, *34*(4), 377–383. https://doi-org.libproxy.chapman.edu/10.1177/00223433970340040

Mair, M. (1988). Psychology as storytelling. *International Journal of Personal Construct Psychology, 3*, 125–137.

Marx, K. (1848/1978). Manifesto of the Communist Party. In R. C. Tucker (Ed.), *The Marx-Engels reader* (pp. 473–500). Norton W. W.

Marx, K. (1856/1978). Speech at the anniversary of the people power. In R. C. Tucker (Ed.), *The Marx-Engels Reader* (pp. 577–578). W. W. Norton.

McIntyre Miller, W. (2016). Toward a scholarship of peace leadership. *International Journal of Public Leadership*, *12*(3), 216–226.

Merton, T. (1976). *On peace*. Redwood Burn.

Merton, T. (2007). *New seeds of contemplation*. New Directions.

Mexiner, C. (2006). Implication of toxic leadership for leadership development: An interview with Jean Lipman-Blumen. *National Clearinghouse for Leadership Programs Concepts and Connections*, *14*(2), 1–4.

Milosevic, I., Maric, S., & Loncar, D. (2020). Defeating the toxic boss: The nature of toxic leadership and the role of followers. *Journal of Leadership & Organizational Studies. 27*(2), 117–137.

Moloney, E., & Williams, M. (2017). *Peace and reconciliation in the classical world*. Routledge.

Moore, T. (1992). *Care of the soul*. Harper Perennial.

Moore, T. (2009). *Writing in the sand*. Hay House.

Mumford, N. D., Zaccaro, S. J., Connelly, M. S., & Marks, M. A. (2000). Leadership skills: Conclusions and future directions. *The Leadership Quarterly*, *11*(1), 155–170.

Nicholls, J. (1994). The 'heart, head, and hands' of transforming leadership. *Leadership & Organization Development Journal*, *15*(6), 8–15.

Nouwen, H. (1994). *Return of the prodigal son: A story of homecoming*. Doubleday.

O'Dea, J. (2012). *Cultivating peace: Becoming a 21st century peace ambassador*. Shift Books.

Oliver, M. (2014). The fourth sign of the zodiac. In *Blue horses* (pp. 61–64). Penguin Books.

Pope Francis. (2016). *Angelus*. www.vatican.va/content/francesco/en/angelus/2016/documents/papa-francesco_angelus_20160306.html

Pope Francis. (2019a). No to the culture of indifference. www.vatican.va/content/francesco/en/cotidie/2019/documents/papa-francesco-cotidie_20190108_notothe-culture-ofindifference.html

Pope Francis. (2019b). Pope's quotes: Virus of indifference. www.ncronline.org/vatican/francis-comic-strip/francis-chronicles/popes-quotes-virus-indifference

Popper, M. (2004). Leadership as relationship. *Journal for the Theory of Social Behaviour, 34*(2), 107–125.

Ricouer, P. (1965). Socius and the neighbour. (C. A. Kelbey, Trans). *History and truth* (pp. 98–109). Northwestern University Press.

Riggio, R. (2011). Introduction: The dialogue of disciplines. In M. Harvey & R. Riggio (Eds.), *Leadership studies: The dialogue of disciplines* (pp. 3–8). Edward Elgar.

Rost, J. (1991). *Leadership for the 21st Century*. Praeger.

Scandura, T. A., & Meuser, J. D. (2022). Relational dynamics of leadership: Problems and prospects. *Annual Review of Organizational Psychology and Organizational Behavior, 9*, 309–337. https://doi.org/10.1146/annurev-orgpsych-012420-091249.

Semple, J. (2023). Who is Vivian Silver? https://globalnews.ca/news/10014375/vivian-silver-israel-attack/

Senge, P. (2006). *The fifth discipline*. Doubleday.

Silver, V. (2018). A Woman Waging Peace. www.womenwagepeace.org.il/en/vivian-silver/

Simmel, G. (1976). Sociability. In *Georg Simmel: Sociologist and European*. (P. A. Lawrence Trans. & Ed.) pp. 57–93. Thomas Nelson.

Simon, P., & Garfunkel, A. (1966). *The sounds of silence*. (youtube.com)

Slovic, P. (2007). 'If I look at the mass I will never act': Psychic numbing and genocide. *Judgment and Decision Making, 2*(2), 79–95.

Staub, ll, R. E. (1997). *The heart of leadership*. Executive Excellence.

Thistle, J. (n.d.). Definition of Indigenous Homelessness in Canada | The Homeless Hub.

Treybig, D. (2016). The prodigal son: Parable with overlooked meaning. *Discern Magazine*. https://lifehopeandtruth.com/change/repentance/the-prodigal-son/

Uhl-Bien, M. (2006). Relational leadership theory: Exploring the social processes of leadership and organizing. *The Leadership Quarterly, 17*(6), 654–676.

UNESCO. (1945). *The UNESCO Courier*. https://unesdoc.unesco.org/ark:/48223/pf0000033223

UNESCO. (n.d.). Building peace in the minds of men and women. https://en.unesco.org/70years/building_peace

United Nations. (2014). UN Official calls on Israeli, Palestinian leaders to make 'difficult compromises' for peace. https://news.un.org/en/story/2014/11/483822

Von Foerster, H. (1990). Ethics and second-order cybernetics. *Opening address for the International Conference, systems and family therapy: Ethics, epistemology, new methods*, Paris, France, 4 October. https://stream.syscoi.com/2018/10/21/ethics-and-second-order-cybernetics-heinz-von-foerster/

Vreja, L. O., Balan, S., & Bosca, L. C. (2016). An evolutionary perspective on toxic leadership. *Management and Economics Review, 1*(2), 217–228.

Watzlawick, P., Wheatland, J. H., & Fisch, R. (1970). *Change: Principles of problem formation and problem resolution.* Norton.

Watzlawick, P. Weakland, J., & Fisch, R. (2011). *Change.* W.W. Norton & Company.

Webb, N. (2011). Paying attention to the musical conversation. *National Association for Musical Education.* https://nafme.org/paying-attention-to-the-musical-conversation/

Weber, M. (1968). *Economy and society: An outline of interpretive sociology.* University of California Press.

Weber, M. (1978). Types of social action. In G. Roth & C. Wittich (Eds.), *Max Weber: Economy and society,* Vol. 1 pp. 24–26. University of California Press.

Welch, M. B. (n.d.). *The Touch of the Master's Hand.* https://barbados.org/poetry/masters.htm.

Wentz, A. (2013). The power of music in storytelling. *Centreline Digital.* www.centerline.net/blog/the-power-of-music-in-storytelling/

World Council of Churches. (2012). *Just peace companion* (2nd Ed.). World Council of Churches.

Yammarino, F. J. (2000). Leadership skills: Introduction and overview. *The Leadership Quarterly, 11*(1), 5–9.

Yukl, G., & Van Fleet, D. D. (1992). Theory and research on leadership in organizations. In M. D. Dunnette & L. M. Hough (Eds.), *Handbook of industrial and organizational psychology* (pp. 147–197). Consulting Psychologists Press.

Zaccaro, S. J. (2007). Trait-based perspectives of leadership. *American Psychologist, 62,* 6–16.

Zimonjic, P. (2023). Trudeau offended Israel with call for 'maximum restraint'. Say Israeli President. www.cbc.ca/news/politics/herzog-says-trudeau-offended-israel-1.7041040

Cambridge Elements ≡

Leadership

in partnership with

Møller Centre, Churchill College
www.mollercentre.co.uk

The Møller Institute (www.mollerinstitute.com), home of the James McGregor Burns Academy of Leadership, brings together business and academia for practical leadership development and executive education. As part of Churchill College in the University of Cambridge, the Institute's purpose is to inspire individuals to be the best they can be, to accelerate the performance of the organizations which they serve, and, through our work, to covenant profits to Churchill College to support the education of future leaders. In everything we do our focus is to create a positive impact for people, society, and the Environment.

International Leadership Association
www.ila-net.org

The International Leadership Association (www.ila-net.org) is the organization for connecting leadership scholars, practitioners, and educators in ways that serve to enhance their learning, their understanding, and their impact in the world. These exchanges are professionally enriching, serve to elevate the field of leadership, and advance our mission to advance leadership knowledge and practice for a better world.

About the Series

Cambridge Elements in Leadership is multi- and inter-disciplinary, and will have broad appeal for leadership courses in Schools of Business, Education, Engineering, Public Policy, and in the Social Sciences and Humanities. In addition to the scholarly audience, Elements appeals to professionals involved in leadership development and training.

The series is published in partnership with the International Leadership Association (ILA) and the Møller Institute, Churchill College in the University of Cambridge.

Printed in the United States
by Baker & Taylor Publisher Services